EMBRACE YOUR OWN
POWER TO FIGHT
CORRUPTION

EMBRACE YOUR OWN POWER TO FIGHT CORRUPTION

BY

S.P. MANCHANDA

Published Internationally by

PENDOWN PRESS

Powered by **Gullybaba Publishing House Pvt. Ltd.,**

An ISO 9001 & ISO 14001 Certified Co.,

Regd. Office: 2525/193, 1st Floor, Onkar Nagar-A, Tri Nagar, Delhi-110035

Ph.: 09350849407, 09312235086

E-mail: info@pendownpress.com

Branch Office: 1A/2A, 20, Hari Sadan, Ansari Road, Daryaganj, New Delhi-110002

Ph.: 011-45794768

Website: PendownPress.com

First Edition: 2020

Price: ₹249/-

ISBN: 978-93-89601-37-4

Layout and Cover Designed by Pendown Graphics Team

Printed and Bound in India by Thomson Press India Ltd.

CONTENTS

Dedicated

to the memory

of

my late wife

Usha Rani Manchanda

For her simplicity

With complete dedication to society

—S.P. Manchanda

FOREWORD

A Pen–Man with the Mission–Possible

After retirement from active life of banker Shri Suraj Parkash Manchanda (67 years) plunged into intensive public activity and soon became social activist. Elders and family members advise the retired to be peaceful and restful. But he considered resting as rusting and rededicated to social cause, for which he used Consumer Protection Act, RTI Act, PIL and grievance redressal mechanisms, which generally are ignored by young and old. He is fighting the corruption with these tools. They are just tools, unfortunately not the weapons. He has also decided to document what he did. And this is that book. It is handbook on fighting for grievances and awakening the sleeping Government machinery and poking the sleeping citizens to wake up the administration from slumber.

The police, with guns are expected to secure the society. Those gun-men are supposed to act as per Law and under instructions from the superiors. But the citizens are expected to be pen-men at least, to use it against abuse of power and corruption. Shri Manchanda is the pen-man. Pen is mightier than gun. It kills the ills and ill wills.

As a pen man he shoots RTI applications against corrupt systems and writes articles to spread awareness. He reminded me that in one of my orders in second appeals I have recorded an appreciation for writing such a constructive RTI request which could curb ultimately the black money generated in immovable properties. The real potential power of RTI could be visualised with such best RTI applications.

One of his great successes is about the exploitation of patients by private hospitals in medical business, which is no more remained a profession. Most of the hospitals are making unethical sometimes criminal profits from selling cardiac stents at a price higher than their import-price, to clear the blockages in the hearts. Shri Manchanda wielded an RTI application that went up to the second appeal in CIC that ultimately leading to capping of the prices of stents the extent of 1/5th the cost charged by hospitals, because he woken up the Govt/National Pharmaceutical Pricing Authority (NPPA) to action. The CIC decision dated 22 February 2017 noted that his success will help so many unfortunate citizens whose loved ones need a cardiac stent but are not able to bear the exorbitant and unreasonable cost that was allowed by lethargic regulatory.

Those who cry from the top of houses that RTI is causing black mail and creating a new profession called RTI Activists who 'abuse' and 'extort', should read this book and talk to this active-author, senior citizen, then they will certainly feel ashamed of what they are propagating. If one Manchanda emerges from each of every five to ten lakh people of India, the administrators shall wake up, politicians with bad motives will pack up and the worse systems will break up.

To ensure the institutionalization of the constitutional values, to realize the mechanisms of good governance and to empower a common man with the power of participating in day-to-day functioning of administration, we need personalities who personify the action and activity, public interest, development and corruption-free system. We need systems. We need enactments like RTI.

I once again record my appreciation for this elder brother of our nation- Shri Suraj Parkash Manchanda, and pray the bright Suraj - SUN to give him strength, health, courage and positive forces so that he will dispel the darkness of corruption with his Parkash of transparency and helps the mankind to achieve corruption-free development. I also would like to make a special mention about the cooperation of his family members, without which, it will be impossible to achieve what he has achieved.

All the best,

M. Sridhar Acharyulu, 23rd December 2019
Former RTI Commissioner, New Delhi

Madabhushi Sridhar Acharyulu is an Indian academic and Ex-Information Commissioner. He was a Professor at Nalsar University of Law in Hyderabad. He's an alumni of the Department of Journalism and Mass Communication at Osmania University.

Disclaimer: The very purpose of this book is to bring awareness to the readers of this book about the rights that they have been given by the Constitution and various Acts which are in place to empower the citizens of this country and help them breathe in an environment which is immune to any kind of corruption and malpractice.

In order to prevent our readers from technical jargons and complexities of words, we have imported materials from various Govt. portals and suitable and authentic sources.

We do not claim that these content are our Intellectual Property and the only purpose for this content to be imported as it is to enlighten our readers, and not otherwise.

ABOUT THE AUTHOR & THE BOOK

Who says activism and wanting to change the society is only for the young and feisty? As we grow older, we see more of the world and have a much more stable view of the world than we did in our early years. This is why seniors with a clear view of the world have a greater chance at making a difference.

Mr Suraj Parkash Manchanda is a 67 year old retired accomplished banker and a devoted social activist. Post his voluntary retirement in 2007; he has dedicated his life for a social cause which includes empowering the senior citizens in India using Consumer Protection Act & RTI Act and most importantly creative writing as a tool to curb corruption. While Acts are enablers, he believes in thoughtful writing to ensure he asks right questions to generate right insights from the responses. He has put his creativity to use in many positive and effective ways and forms:

- **Writing Public Grievances:** Time, courage and serious thinking along-with creative writing are only necessary funding required for mission of fighting corruption and irregularities through power of pen. He is not just writing public-grievances himself but also enabling and educating other citizens including elderly people on art of writing powerful complaints, public grievances and RTI-applications.

- **Writing RTI Applications:** His art of using RTI Act as a tool to plug loopholes and corruption in system is being keenly observed and appreciated in judicial, legislative and bureaucratic circles. He has written hundreds of RTI-petitions on many issues like corruption, black money in immovable properties, cardiac stent prices, MRP of essential drugs, medical negligence etc. CIC verdicts on his public-interest RTI petitions are automatically picked up by media because of importance of issues involved in his petitions.

- **Filing Public Interest Petitions:** After getting desired information under RTI Act, he becomes busy to file public interest litigation (PIL) in the High Court of Delhi in larger public interest issues. He has filed PIL against summer vacations in courts when doors of the judiciary are closed for litigants while officers and advocates of the court enjoy summers in air-conditioned rooms or at hill stations. A PIL was also filed against use of English only in the High Courts and Supreme Court of India whereas Hindi knowing litigant is not allowed fighting his own case and defending himself. He has also filed PIL in Delhi High Court against irrational government minimum rates (circle rates) of immovable properties which encourage corruption and black money transactions. The High Court has issued Notice to the Govt of NCT of Delhi and counsel for the respondent govt admitted anomalies. We will soon get revised circle rates calculated on scientific basis.

- **Educating fellow senior citizens:** He conducts multiple sessions/workshops at different forums on Consumer Protection Act & RTI Act and their applications. He also provides personal guidance to people who are facing a concern that can potentially be resolved using Public-Grievance-Monitoring-System managed by Central and State Governments.

Mr. Manchanda spends 2-3 hours time every day for writing public grievances/complaints/suggestions, because the passion to use pen-power against corruption is his only hobby. This also means taking out time of his normal business-schedule to attend hearings at Central Information Commission, Courts and members of public organised by educational institutions, RWAs and NGOs. He is not only filing complaints/RTI-petitions to pull up public authorities for their wrong-doings, but have also filed many public-grievances with the CMO, PMO, Department of Administrative Reforms & Public Grievance and public-interest-litigations (PIL) in the High Court of Delhi after obtaining desired information under RTI Act.

Some of his key achievements are as follows:

- Many government-departments and public-authorities implemented suitable reforms after irregularities and malpractices were exposed through his RTI-petitions, grilling concerned departments and ministries on various matters. On 01.10.2015 (International Day of Older Persons), Hon'ble Chief Minister of Delhi honoured him as one of the best senior citizens doing social service for the care and welfare of elderly people.

- He has written many articles on use of RTI Act which has gained attention of concerned ones, and also be highlighted in media as well as on the CIC website. In one of its judgments dated 9th January 2015 Hon'ble CIC observed his petition to curb black money in immovable properties as one of the best RTI-applications in the interest of fulfilling the objectives of Right to Information Act.

- When he came to know that hospitals were making huge profits from selling cardiac stents at a price much more than import-price to treat blockages in the heart, he filed many complaints, RTIs and appeal to CIC which finally led to the Govt / National Pharmaceutical Pricing Authority (NPPA) to cap the prices of stents to 1/5th the cost charged by hospitals. According to CIC decision dated 22 Feb. 2017, his success will help so many unfortunate citizens whose loved ones are in need of a cardiac stent but are not able to bear the exaggerated cost. The Commission finally appreciated the applicant for having espoused a cause of larger public interest.

- He filed many complaints/grievances and RTI on the issue of high MRP of oncology medicines. Serious issues such as reducing the cost of cancer medicines and generic medicines were heard by the Central Information Commission. CIC advised the Ministry of Health & Family Welfare and Department of Pharmaceutical NPPA to check menace of overpricing of drugs and make effective combined efforts to address this issue. Finally MRP of 390 non-scheduled cancer medicines were reduced by upto 87 percent, which would result in annual saving of Rs.800 crore for the patients (Economic Times 08.03.2019).

- There is lot of corruption and black money in property transactions due to illogical, irrational and arbitrarily fixed circle rates in Delhi. He filed many complaints, grievances, RTI-applications and PIL in the High Court of Delhi to force the government to recalculate circle rates in a scientific manner. Honourable Chief Justice of Delhi High Court issued Notice to Govt of NCT of Delhi on 14.5.2019 and 03.09.2019. He forced the government to revise circle rates to substantially reduce corruption in real estate dealings.

At present, he is the Vice-President of Elderly People's Forum, Keshav Puram Delhi having more than 800 members on its roll. He is also President and Convener-Trustee of registered non-government organisation, Prakash-India, established with the aim of consumer awareness, environment protection and combat corruption in India. He is also associated with Transparency International (India) and Akhil Bhartiya Grahak Panchayat, working for consumer protection in India. He has been a source of inspiration for the senior citizens who have sufficient experience and time to write complaints/grievances/RTI-applications as a tool to decrease corruption and cure lethargy in public functioning in India.Further he is motivating people, his fellow senior citizens in particular, to donate eyes and other organs after death. He spreads awareness, motivates, registers the pledges for body/organs donation and co-ordinates the donation between his family and the medical institutions after the death of donor. He also encourages CNG/Electric cremation instead of traditional cremation to save environment.

The author has dealt with many important aspects of life that determine our success and failure. He is of the opinion that it is very important to understand the ground realities, the truth of practical life. It is hoped that his wonderful gesture of sacrificing a lucrative career to guide fellow senior citizens and the next generation will meet with great success. The book makes an interesting reading and Mr. Manchanda has attempted to address all relevant issues in an informal manner that is bound to appeal to all his readers.

The real beauty of this book is that one can follow the simple route the author has formulated to lead a helpful social life. One just has to understand and be aware of the issues & problems and simple way of solution as discussed by him. It is not a bad bargain to have a peaceful and successful life by just spending 1-2 hours every day as per his suggestions. After a few months you won't have to spend even an hour daily, if you constantly feel aware of the issues discussed by him and method of writing grievances/ complaints/ RTIs/PILs to the authorities for redress.

—Publisher

INTRODUCTION

PURPOSE OF WRITING THE BOOK

India is undoubtedly one of the attractive places on this earth. Its natural and cultural wealth is a great centre of attraction for many. However, the greatness and goodwill of our nation is spoilt by the corrupt activities which go on unabashedly. Corruption is one such problem which has been prevalent in our country since ages. Dishonesty of the people in power and bribery at various levels is what leads to ever-increasing corruption in our country.

Fodder Scam (Rs 950 Crore), Stock Market Scam (Rs 4000 Crore), Satyam Scam (Rs 7000 Crore), Stamp Paper Scam (Rs 43000 Crore), Commonwealth Games Scam (Rs 70,000 Crore), 2G Spectrum Scam (1 Lakh 67 thousand crore rupees), Foodgrain scam (2 lakh crore rupees) the list goes on and on.

> **Have we ever thought about the probable reason for such level of corruption?**

The most common reason is that corrupt people think they can get away with it because:

We only read all these scams from the perspective of news and then gradually forget them.

We stay silent and don't seek answers from such corrupt people

We are not even concerned about corrupt politics or tarnished images of running candidates

We stay ignorant and easy going as long as things don't impact us directly

One can say there are many types of laws that have also been prescribed to completely eliminate corruption from the country. There are many anti-corruption acts being passed by the government to address this situation, such as Right to Information Act 2005; Prevention of Money Laundering Act, 2002; Prosecution Section of Income Tax Act, 1961; Indian Penal Code, 1860, etc. It depends on the government officials and of course the people of our country how they act upon these preventive measures and immediately report to the police or the concerned authority of any unlawful activity that takes place right under our nose.

Having said that eradicating corruption is more than just enacting laws. Is taking and giving bribe not a crime? Is there no law against dowry? Yes, but dowry is still ongoing in our society under our nose and bribes are still taken and given. Officially enacted rules / laws can curb corruption in the society to an extent, but the society needs to take charge and embrace its own power to fight corruption. Corruption can be curbed and brought to an end if and only if every Indian citizen do not choose to run away from his/her conscience and vows to build corruption free India on the sound, moral principles and ethical values for which India was known since ages.

It is possible in the boundaries of our home by using anti-corruption laws such as RTI Act and by asking questions from the corrupt authorities using government portals. RTI is a very strong tool to improve or bring transparency in the functioning of government and official works. We are also constantly supported by both technology and media to spread awareness and messages amongst the millions of population within no time. So unleash its power and work towards it because if you aren't affected today, you'll be affected in the days to come.Nothing is impossible if we believe in ourselves and work with all our strength towards realizing that goal – whether it's our personal objectives or making India a peaceful haven to live in and rejoice.

I know my limitation in the ocean of knowledge and activism. I am also sure that many of you are much more knowledgeable and more active than me. I have just tried to make a humble effort to share my experiences as RTI activist and an active social worker working for the welfare of community. Fortunately a few years back I realized that the life had given me more than I deserved and desired, so I thought of doing my bit as a token of acknowledgement of this debt. I wondered how best one could serve the cause of millions not getting fairness because of lethargic attitude of government officials and rampant corruption in the system. I tried to analyze cause of unhappiness in our country and came to the conclusion that throughout my country easy-going attitude of authorities and corruption in our society are the real causes of common people's sadness. The people would love to combat corruption but would depend on some 'Anna Hazare' to come forward and sit on hunger strike for them.

Having learnt about the law of impermanence and that no one is indispensible; one should not be satisfied to live an idle or routine life. The real purpose of life to help society can be achieved best only if we are established in self. Routine help to society and reasonably balanced life can be lived with ordinary life style. In every society majority of population is busy in earning a living and attending day-today routine things or enjoying life with friends. Although many people feel concerned and try to do their bit yet only a handful of blessed people have the strength and wisdom to do something big and constructive for the welfare of society. But for the realization and the capacity to make a big difference would come only if we conquer all the enemies within. Only when people love and respect your ideas and personality would you be able to change the world around you. We must have conviction that we can change the world. Once a person attains that level of evolvement, one can with a simple article arouse sentiments, which can lead to protests and even a revolution. So prepare yourself for the bigger mission in life which is possible only if we do all that is essential to avoid all those things which are obstructions to our big mission. Humanity is suffering not because of greed of corrupt but because of silence of honest people.

It is true that no one can solve all the problems of the world. I am not even saying that one should lose sleep or peace of mind because of these problems. One should not even depress about these problems. But surely one should be sensitive and conscious of the problems. If one is sensitive to others' problems, one would get many opportunities to serve mankind. One could help in many small ways to make a big difference to the person one is helping. I am also not suggesting that to start with one should neglect his personal or professional responsibility in order to do social service. Just spending few hours a week doing some selfless work is sufficient to initiate one into this blissful path. As you reach out to more and more people and help them solve their problems, you will gradually develop the instinctive ability to speak on matters that the other person wants to discuss. The sense of fulfillment you get by spending time on such opportunities would also make you feel more at peace with yourself.

We have all experienced that often we are stuck with some issue or problem and twenty-four hours of the day, week after week, that issue keeps bothering us. We should always keep in mind that irrespective of any issue we have to devote time to some day-to-day activities of life that a balanced person cannot even afford to be obsessed all the time with one problem. We have to spend some time for our personal needs, some for professional activity and have to attend to some social and welfare activities as well.

Every person should spend at least few hours for any social service project. We do not have to disturb our normal routine for this. One could participate in a discussion about some social or corruption problem in our society. One should be sensitive to problems and should do whatever we can. One can write an article giving one's suggestions or just send e-mail to the concerned person on some issue or write grievance/RTI-application to the concerned authority. One may visit an NGO and ask if she/he could assist them in their noble mission. Just do your bit to fulfill your sense of social responsibility. What's more, when you do something meaningful, you do more than just change the world.

When you feel strongly about an issue that doesn't get enough attention or where change is very slow, become educated on the issue and what's being done to address it. Then you can highlight the issue, write complaint to government, file RTI-application, and share information with your friends and family. You can do it through modern social media, and even by writing good old-fashioned letters to your government representatives and/or file formal grievance on government portals. Working on an issue like this, you can create a huge impact. Either write things worth reading or Do things worth the writing.

CHAPTER 1

PUBLIC GRIEVANCE FILING SYSTEM

COMPLAINT REDRESS MECHANISM

Imagine a situation where you are going to a government organization for as pecific work.

But employees are not helping to pass your file with out bribe.

Now you are helpless and don't know to whom you should complaint.

What do you do in such situations? We only know of two options – You pay the bribe to get things done or wait indefinitely at a mercy of government staff.

There is a third option–Government Official Grievance Portals. These online portals have been introduced for redressal of any sort of complaint a common citizen may have. It allows you to reach out to concerned authority and raise a voice against a corrupt practice that you may have encountered while interacting with any government department at central and state level. The type of complaint/grievance can vary from work not getting done, irresponsible behavior of staff or any other social issue that you believe needs attention.

The process of filing the complaint/grievance involves some easy steps:

- Log on to the portal and share the grievance as simple text

- After providing details of your name, address, mobile number and email ID, you may write your grievance/complaint to the concerned department.

- These grievances are then allocated to the concerned authorities for an official response

- Registration number will be issued to track and monitor the response

- After some days you will get phone call and will be asked if the work is done and that you are satisfied or not

- If you are not satisfied, the matter will be again referred to the authority for taking up the matter satisfactorily

- If satisfied, you may give your feedback/remarks

    Embrace Your Own Power to Fight Corruption

Online petition filing and Monitoring System

Quick Links for reference:

Link	Go here….
https://pgportal.gov.in/	…when issue is related to central government
https://pgms.delhi.gov.in	…when issue is a Delhi state issue
https://dpg.gov.in/	…when you are not happy with response and would like to escalate to Directorate of Public Grievances (DPG)
http://listeningpostdelhilg.in/	…when you have to reach out to LG of Delhi
https://pmopg.gov.in/pmocitizen/Grievancepmo.aspx	…when you need attention of Prime Minister's office
https://helpline.rb.nic.in/	…when you want to reach President's Secretariat Helpline

Through these online grievance portals you can mention problems in simple words to the concerned officers/department in a systematic manner to get desired solution. As per the procedure of the online grievance portal, every effort is made to solve almost all the problems as soon as possible. All these above mentioned portals provided for social benefits may be used by the common citizen of India for grievance solving. For inspiration, you can find some examples of many grievances that I have personally lodged in public interest for an effectiveness and efficiency of government operations. Please find more details of the factual grievances and authorities response in the following pages.

MCD not included in online RTI portal

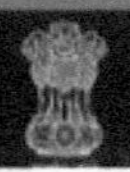

Grievance Status

Grievance No	2019012102
Date of Grievance	24/10/2019
Complainant Name	S.P. Manchanda
Contact Nos.	(LandLine),9891827669(Mobile)
Category	Online Entry by Citizen ::
Complainant Address	C-2/35 B, Keshav Puram, Delhi 110035

Grievance Details

We welcome Delhi government decision to allow filing of RTI application online for greater transparency. But it is disappointing to note that Municipal Corporation of Delhi is not in the list. Whereas we can file public grievance to MCD North/East/West on line, it is beyond understanding why these departments are not included in the list for filing RTI application to get information which may help us to know the working of MCD. Previously before trifurcation, we used to file online RTI petitions, but after 2011 this facility has been withdrawn from us. Website shows still under construction. Action Required : Please direct the Govt of NCT of Delhi and MCD to restart online filing of RTI applications through MCD North website at the earliest and poivide us list of PIOs and FAA.

Grievance Site Address C2/35 B, Keshav Puram, Delhi 110035

Departmental User	Locality	Action Taken	Status	Contact Details
NORTH DMC	Keshav Puram	22/11/2019 Online RTI Application has been started on 18/11/2019	Over	Sh. Asad Parvez Addl. Director (IT) 23227418 addldirectoritndmc@mcd.gov.in

***

Road-side unauthorized construction of temple should be stopped

Grievance Status

Grievance No	2017102172
Date of Grievance	13/12/2017
Complainant Name	Suraj Parkash
Contact Nos.	(LandLine),9891827669(Mobile)
Category	Online Entry by Citizen ::
Complainant Address	President, Elderly People Forum, C4 block, Keshav Puram, Delhi 110035

Grievance Details

We would like to complaint that there is pukka construction of unauthorized temple started at the main road towards the C7 market between C4 and C7 blocks, which is illegal and should be stopped immediately because it will reduce the road breadth causing traffic jams and pollution in the area. Kindly take action at the earliest in interest of surrounding public.

Grievance Site Address: Road between C4 block and C7 block

Department   MCD NORTH

Action Taken   21/12/2017

The site has been inspected and it has been found that the addition/ alternation work in old existing mandir was found progress at site. However, the same was stop during inspection.

Contact Details

Sh. K.K. Sharma,

Executive Engineer M II

01127305387, eemiikpz@gmail.com

Embrace Your Own Power to Fight Corruption

DGEHS retired senior citizens seek Ayurvedic treatment without prior approval from government hospitals

Grievance Status

Grievance No	2018085205
Date of Grievance	28/07/2018
Complainant Name	Suraj Parkash Manchanda
Contact Nos.	(LandLine),9891827669(Mobile)
Category	Online Entry by Citizen ::
Complainant Address	Block C 2, Flat No. 35 B
	Keshav Puram, Delhi 110035
E-Mail ID	suraj_1511@yahoo.com

Grievance Details

This is a public grievance, more particularly grievance of senior citizens/pensioners, who retired from departments and organisations of Govt of NCT of Delhi and got DGEHS cards for treatment from Allopathic/AYUSH hospitals and centers in the city. As per rules, the treatment at all empaneled AYUSH Hospitals / Centers may be taken ONLY with the PRIOR authorization/permission from government hospitals at the time of taking treatment whereas no such prior permission is required if the treatment is taken in some empaneled allopathic hospital. This creates hardships to those senior citizens who prefer Ayurveda line of treatment. Further during treatment at Ayurveda/AYUSH hospital if elderly people are diagnosed with some other disease/s, they are asked to go to government hospital again for taking permission for treatment of those newly diagnosed disease/s which only adds sufferings to them. The Delhi government should amend the rules to allow treatment to all senior citizen DGEHS card holders who prefer Ayurveda medicines from empaneled AYUSH hospitals and centers, without prior authorization/permission from government hospitals as in case of empaneled allopathic hospitals and dispensaries.

Grievance Site Address: Block C 2, Flat No. 35
B Keshav Puram, Delhi 110035

Department Director Health Services

Action Taken 20/09/2019

As per order 01/8/19, for availing ayush treatment from empaneled centres, need of prior authorization as been done away.

Contact Details

Dr. Deepak Kumar Singh,
Addl. Director (DGEHS)
22391435, sopdgehs@gmail.com

     Embrace Your Own Power to Fight Corruption

Deficient service at post office Keshav Puram, Delhi

CPGRAMS New
Centralized Public Grievance Redress And Monitoring System

Grievance Status for registration number: DPOST/E/2016/10812

GRIEVANCE CONCERNS TO

Name of Complainant	SP Manchanda
Date of Receipt	05/09/2016
Received By Ministry/Department	Posts

Grievance Description

A large number of senior citizens as well as other public members have brought to our notice that both the above names post offices are not functioning properly for the last two weeks due to online-system. This is not the first instance but the customers are being badly harassed for the last about ten months since the introduction of online system buy the Department of Posts. The following difficulties are being brought to your notice:

1. Most to the senior citizens have opened their accounts such as MIS and Senior Citizen accounts. Their source of income is only the interest on their fixed accounts opened in the post offices and banks. If interest on their fixed deposits is not paid on due dates it can be imagined how they are running their lives.

2. The retired personnel are drawing their monthly pension through post offices. Due to non-functioning of the online-system of post offices, they are not getting their pension when they need most.

3. Similar is the position with other customers for getting transactions/payments of small saving schemes of post offices.

I would like to mention that besides being harassed by the valuable customers of the post offices, the Department of Posts is also losing the business. For example some of the members of our association have also brought to our notice that due to unsatisfactory service being provided by the post offices they have transferred their PPF and saving accounts to different banks. Due to introduction of new hopeless online-system, all kinds of services are not being provided by the post offices satisfactorily as the online-system generally remains out of order or the staff is not competent to adjust to it.

Sir, I would like to inform your good self that this is not the first time that we are bringing the matter to your kind notice, but the complaints/grievances have been brought to the notice of concerned Divisional Heads as well as the Head of Circle, but extremely sorry to say that the authority concerned are least bothered to solve the grievances/problems of the public seriously with the result that the public is suffering poorly and the Department of Posts is also losing business as also the creditability. Govt. of India is giving publicity that the post offices will be paying bank from the coming financing year. If the things remain the same we are doubtful whether Department of Post will be in a position to give satisfactory services at par with the banking services provided by public sector banks and private banks in India.

At the end I would request your honour that the authority concerned may be directed to take the public grievance seriously and get the things in a right way so that all the customers get rid of all the difficulties and problems as explained above.

  Embrace Your Own Power to Fight Corruption

Current Status	Case closed
Date of Action	20/09/2016
Remarks	

There is a technical problem of internet connectivity at Keshav Puram Post office, due to which CBS online module is not functioning properly. Complaint has been lodged with the network service provider and is expected to be resolved soon.

OFFICER CONCERNS TO

Officer Name	**Umesh Kumar**
Officer Designation	SPOs Delhi North Dn.
Contact Address	
Email Address	dodelhinorth.dl@indiapost.gov.in
Contact Number	01123814630

***

Government issuing large-sized currency notes disproportionate to new notes

CPGRAMS New
Centralized Public Grievance Redress And Monitoring System

Grievance Status for registration number: DARPG/E/2017/02867

GRIEVANCE CONCERNS TO

Name Of Complainant	Suraj Parkash
Date of Receipt	05/02/2017
Received By Ministry/Department	
	Department of Administrative Reforms and Public Grievances

Grievance Description

This refers to media-reports about Reserve Bank of India (RBI) issuing new series of rupees 100 notes with same design but with signature of new RBI governor Urjit Patel. Earlier new series of currency-notes of rupees 20 and 50 were issued as per RBI notification dated 04.12.2016 which were equal in sizes and similar in design to earlier currency-notes of respective same denominations, except for some light colour of front portions of these notes due to change in print-procedure and signed by new RBI governor Urjit R Patel.

I have to submit that issuance of large-sized notes of rupees 20, 50 and 100 will be disproportionate to small-sized new currency-notes of rupees 500 and 2000. New notes in denominations of rupees 20, 50, 100 should be issued in smaller sizes than earlier ones with designs in tune with newly issued rupees-500 notes. Since currency-crunch is gradually coming to an end, any further printing of 2000-rupees notes should be stopped as soon as possible. Rather currency-notes of 200/250-rupees denominations should be printed as per widely accepted international practice in respect of denominations of currency-notes.

Current Status	Case closed
Date of Action	19/07/2017
Remarks	noted

OFFICER CONCERNS TO

Officer Name	**Manmohan Sachdeva**
Officer Designation	Director
Contact Address	Room No. North Block
	New Delhi
Email Address	mm.sachdeva@nic.in
Contact Number	23093810

 Embrace Your Own Power to Fight Corruption

Menace of cola-drinks and junk food in India

 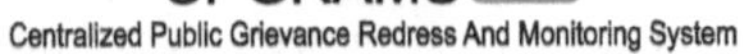 

Grievance Status for registration number:

DHLTH/E/2017/01769

GRIEVANCE CONCERNS TO

Name Of Complainant   Suraj Parkash Manchanda

Date of Receipt   05/03/2017

Received By Ministry/Department

Health & Family Welfare

Grievance Description

I would like to share some of the initiatives taken by a group of knowledgeable senior citizens of this Forum in the area of 'The Truth about Carbonated Drinks and Junk Food'. Some of the major findings emanating from these initiatives are given below:

1. A majority of soft drinks manufacturers use large amounts of sugar as preservative to increase the shelf life. 43% of added sugars in our diet come from sweetened beverages. One Can of soft drink averages eight teaspoons of sugar as preservative, which is very bad for teeth, heart diabetes, kidneys etc.

2. Cola-drinks and junk food with high levels of sugar, fat and salt, is a major cause of non-communicable diseases in India. As per WHO (2011), with over 52 lakh deaths in India in 2008, non-communicable diseases have become number one killer in the country. Unhealthy diets and lack

of physical activity are also key risk factors for major non-communicable diseases such as cardiovascular diseases (CAD), cancer and diabetes.

3. A normal outing at McDonalds which usually involves munching on an order of French fries, a burger and sipping on a cola-drink will set us back by around 1100 calories. Severe lack of nutrition, coupled with high chemical, high sodium amid high preservative contents makes it quite an 'Unhappy Meal'

4. New study indicates pesticides 24 times higher than Bureau of Indian Standards norms. The Center for Science and Environment (CSE) recently came out with a new report on the levels of pesticides in soft drinks available in the market. The report indicated the presence of 5 different pesticides in all the samples, 24 times higher than the Bureau of Indian Standards (BIS) norms, which have been finalized but not yet notified. The latest study is based on tests conducted on 57 samples of 11 soft drink brands from 25 different manufacturing plants of Coca-Cola and Pepsico, spread over 12 States.

5. Some of the cola-companies voluntarily stopped selling cola-drinks in schools worldwide in view of increasing obesity in school-going children. Some states in India including Tamil Nadu and Kerala have also stopped sale of cola-drinks. Quite recently, Nagaland government on 14.03.2017 banned sale of junk food and soft drinks both on school campuses as well as in a radius of 200 meters from each school.

6. In response to RTI-application, Northern Railway Catering Unit informed about a strict ban on supply

     Embrace Your Own Power to Fight Corruption

and sale of all kind of soft drinks like Pepsi-Cola, Coca-cola, mirinda orange, mirinda lemon, 7-up, fanta, limca, sprite, thums-up, mountain dew, diet pepsi, blue pepsi, etc. and all other brands of drinks of these nature in the Parliament House from 06.08.2003. Even it ordered the agencies to immediately remove display-refrigerators and advertisement-materials of soft drinks on orders of the Chairman of Joint Parliamentary Committee on Food Management in Parliament House Complex. If such a ban is imposed in Parliament House complex, then these drinks should also be banned for general public in larger public interest. After all public-health must not be considered less important than of Parliamentarians and others using Parliament canteens.

7. As a part of social life, people all over the world love to drink cola-drinks because of its unique tangy taste, but if they are properly informed about the contents of colas and its harmful effects on their health, they would immediately stop using it.

    We, in Elderly People Forum, have been taking up issues relating to health and well being of our future generations. In the interest of national health, we as well-informed citizens of this country humbly request you to kindly take adequate measures promptly to safeguard the health of all citizens of this nation from the menace of cola-drinks and junk food in a mission mode.

    Current Status   Case closed

    Date of Action   23/03/2017

Remarks

The complainant has been communicated/replied vide letter

No. 11(1)2016/Grievance/Enf/FSSAI. Dated 22nd Mar, 2017.
Copy of the same is attached.

OFFICER CONCERNS TO

Officer Name	**Shri Raj Singh**
Officer Designation	Head GA
Contact Address	FDA Bhawan, Kotla Road, New Delhi
Email Address	r.singh@nic.in
Contact Number	23230997

File No. 11(1)2016/Grievance/Enf/FSSAI
Food Safety and Standards Authority of India
(A Statutory Authority established under the Food Safety & Standards Act, 2006)
(Regulatory Compliance Division)
FDA Bhawan, Kotla Road, New Delhi-110 002

Dated, the 22 March, 2017

To

Sh. Suraj Parkash Manchanda,
President, M/s Elderly People Forum,
C2-35 B, Keshav Puram,
Delhi-110035.

Subject: Grievance petition vide DHLTH/E/2017/01769 dated 15.03.2017- reg.

Sir,

Please refer to your grievance No. DHLTH/E/2017/01769 dated 15.03.2017 regarding safeguarding the health of people of nation from cola drinks and junk food in a mission mode.

2. In this regard, you are informed that mandate of FSS Act, 2006 is to provide safe and wholesome food for the human consumption. "Cold Drinks" are covered under "Non-alcoholic Carbonated Beverages" for which the standards have been prescribed through Sub-Regulation 2.10.6 of the Food Safety and Standards (Food Products Standards and Food Additives) Regulations, 2011 and the Food Business Operators (FBOs) have to adhere to the same.

3. Further, Food Safety and Standards Authority of India have also issued draft guidelines titled 'Guidelines for making available wholesome, nutritious, safe and hygienic food to school children in India' and restricting/limiting availability of Food high in Fat, Sugar and Salt (HFSS Foods) among school children which is uploaded on FSSAI's official website. Junk Food is not defined under the Food Safety and Standards Act, 2006 and Rules and Regulations made thereunder.

4. Additionally, concerns expressed in your grievance petition regarding safe food and public healths are very thoughtful and the suggestions mentioned have been noted by this office. We appreciate your efforts and awareness being a consumer for the public interest.

(Anupam Rastogi)
Assistant Director (Sur. / IT)

 Embrace Your Own Power to Fight Corruption

Super-costly medicines used for treatment of various cancer-patients

 प्रशासनिक सुधार और लोक शिकायत विभाग
DEPARTMENT OF ADMINISTRATIVE
REFORMS & PUBLIC GRIEVANCES

CPGRAMS New
Centralized Public Grievance Redress And Monitoring System

Grievance Status for registration number :
DPHAM/E/2017/00109

GRIEVANCE CONCERNS TO

Name Of Complainant   S P Manchanda

Date of Receipt   14/04/2017

Received By Ministry/Department   Pharmaceutical

Grievance Description

At a time when certain surgeons, private hospitals, and chemists left no stone unturned in minting money through an unregulated sale-price of stents used in heart-ailments, central government indeed did a great service to mankind by regulating prices of stents.

Now immediate focus of the central government should be on regulating prices of super-costly medicines used for treatment of various cancer-patients. A study made at wholesale medicine-market of Bhagirath Palace and South Delhi reveals that oncology-medicines required for treating cancer have Maximum-Retail-Price (MRP) which is many times of their import-price or ex-factory price with profit-margins several hundred times. Cancer is one such expensive disease which requires such super-costly medicines on daily basis for several months or even years. National Pharmaceutical Pricing Authority (NPPA) should make an urgent study of mode of pricing medicines required used to treat cancer at different hospitals in India, and direct drug-manufacturing-companies for reasonable ex-factory price of these medicines. Also big gap between ex-factory price and MRP of oncology-medicines should be reduced to be a reasonable one just like cardiac stents now sold at reasonable prices.

Current Status   Case closed

Date of Action   20/11/2017

Remarks

Your grievance has been taken note of and National Pharmaceutical Pricing Authority (NPPA) has been instructed to look into the issue.

OFFICER CONCERNS TO

Officer Name   **Ms. Ritu Dhillon**

Officer Designation   Member Secretary

Contact Address   3rd/5th Floor, YMCA Cultural Center Building 1, Jai Singh Road, New Delhi

Email Address

Contact Number   01123746649

High MRP of oncology medicines to be reduced

 प्रशासनिक सुधार और लोक शिकायत विभाग
DEPARTMENT OF ADMINISTRATIVE
REFORMS & PUBLIC GRIEVANCES

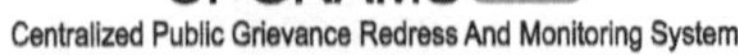 **CPGRAMS** New
Centralized Public Grievance Redress And Monitoring System

Grievance Status for registration number:
PMOPG/E/2018/0588637

GRIEVANCE CONCERNS TO

Name Of Complainant   **Suraj Parkash Manchanda**

Date of Receipt   27/12/2018

Received By Ministry/Department   Prime Ministers Office

Grievance Description

This refers to order of Second Appeal No. CIC/NPPAT/A/2017/152869-BJ of my RTI application, under which some of the oncology medicines that are required in the treatment of cancer had MRP printed which was many times more than their ex-factory price or import price. I have filed many complaints/grievances on this issue but the Ministry of Health and Family Welfare/Department of Pharmaceutical NPPA has not yet taken suitable constructive action in this regard. Serious issues such as reducing the cost of these cancer medicines and generic medicines were heard by the CIC. As a final decision of the appeal, the Information Commissioner Mr. BimalJulka has found that major problems related to price structure and extraordinary huge business margins especially on cancer medicines generic medicines, have yet to be resolved by the Department of Pharmaceutical and NPPA. The Commission advised the Health and Family Welfare / Department of Pharmaceutical NPPA to make effective combined efforts to address this issue. Along withrecommendations, CIC also advised that within a period of two months the decision has to be taken jointly by all stakeholders to benefit the larger public. Due to excessive margins between the ex-factory price and MRP of medicines specially used in the treatment of cancer, promotes corruption. Many MRP of medicines have been regulated by the Dept/NPPA, but many medicines are still there on which the printed value is much-much higher than their production value. Two months have passed for this CIC decision, but no instructions or suggestions from any relevant department or ministry seems to have been implemented related to this issue. Considering CICs recommendation, Health and Family Welfare/Department of Pharmaceutical NPPA need to take serious decisions on reducing the cost of oncology medicine and many more medicines needs price regulation. There is an urgent requirement to decide constructive rules to control the high MRP of medicines. Due to the reduction of the cost of medicines, many troubled patients will receive financial and psychological support. The action taken by all relevant in the period of last two months period provided by the Information Commissioner should be provided to the information commissioner and the appellant also as soon as possible.

The above mentioned grievance DPHAM/E/2018/00272 was filed on 3.12.2018 after obtaining information under RTI Act. While disposing of the grievance on 27.12.2018, the Deputy Director, Pharmaceutical Deptt stated that "at present there is no provision under DPCO-2013 by which the trade margin of drugs can be regulated. The issue relating to price structure of medicines and trade margins in medicines is a policy matter..." We request the competent authorities to amend the said policy in larger public interest so that we are not cheated by pharmaceutical companies, chemists and hospitals who sell medicines at exorbitant MRPs.

 Embrace Your Own Power to Fight Corruption

Current Status	Case closed
Date of Action	15/01/2019
Remarks	

We are thankful to you for taking timeout for giving us valuable suggestion. The Department has taken note of your suggestion. Policy formulation is a complex process and it requires consultation with a variety of stakeholders. The issue of Trade Margin rationalization is under consideration of the Department.

GRIEVANCE CONCERNS TO

Officer Name	**Remya Prabha**
Officer Designation	Deputy Director
Contact Address	Room No.235, A-wing,
	Shastri Bhawan, New Delhi
Email Address	remya.prabha@gov.in
Contact Number	23071162

Huge unclaimed deposits in banks need regulation

Grievance Status for registration number :

DARPG/E/2017/13169

GRIEVANCE CONCERNS TO

Name Of Complainant   Suraj Parkash Manchanda

Date of Receipt   25/05/2017

Received By Ministry/Department

Department of Administrative Reforms and Public Grievances

Grievance Description

Crores of rupees are lying in inoperative accounts in banks with even many account-holders having forgotten about their bank-accounts. Reserve Bank of India (RBI) has introduced 'Know Your Customer' (KYC) forms which has been made mandatory also for closing such inoperative accounts. Such cumbersome practice not only is causing difficulty to account-holders wishing to close their inoperative accounts, but also creating a big loss of man-hours of bank-employees apart from unnecessary data-entries and record-keeping. Frauds are reported through some bank-employees misappropriating funds in such inoperative accounts where amount is large.

RBI/IBA should direct all banks to close all accounts not operated for say last three years, and send the remittance through pay-orders by Speed Post at last-known addresses of account-holders at least for accounts having balance of say rupees five

 Embrace Your Own Power to Fight Corruption

thousand or less. In case of return of Speed-Post envelopes, formalities like of KYC form and succession-certificates etc may be required. For amounts bigger than rupees five thousand, account-holders should be informed about their existing balance and to approach banks either to make accounts operative or close these in a time-bound period after which all such balances should be transferred to 'Depositor Educative Awareness Fund' (DEAF) Time-limit for transfer of funds to 'DEAF' should be reduced to three years from present unreasonable ten years. With private sector dominating banking sector, public-money lying in inoperative accounts must not be allowed to be retained and used by banks for profiteering.

Current Status   Case closed

Date of Action   12/09/2017

Remarks

Also Refer DBOD.No.Leg.BC.34/09.07.005/2008-09 dt 22-08-08 DBOD.No.Leg.BC.45/C.466(IV)/89 November 15, 1989 The Chairman of All Public Sector Banks Dear Sirs, Customer Service- Estimates Committee-64th Report The Estimates Committee in its 64th Report had observed that in spite of the introduction of Nomination facilities and Reserve Bank of India instructions to settle claims upto Rs. 25,000/- without insisting on succession certificate etc., large amounts of deposits made by account holders who have made no nominations are being held up in banks as dormant accounts. The matter has been considered by the Government and Reserve Bank of India and it has been decided that banks' branches should follow up accounts which remain inoperative for a year or so by sending suitable advices to the customers and if the said letters are returned undelivered they may immediately be put on enquiry to find out the whereabouts of customers or their legal heirs in case they are deceased. Such prompt follow up might enable the banks and the legal heirs where applicable to take such steps as are necessary to change the status of the accounts and would also reduce the quantum of unclaimed deposits with the banks both in regard to amount and number. You are requested to issue suitable instructions to your branches under advice to us. Yours faithfully, Sd/ (K. L. Batra) Joint Chief Officer.

OFFICER CONCERNS TO

Officer Name	**Shri Saurav Sinha**
Officer Designation	Chief General Manager InCharge
Contact Address	Reserve Bank of India
	Central Office Building,
	Fort Mumbai
Email Address	cgmicdbr@rbi.org.in
Contact Number	02222701223

Irrational Circle Rates of immovable properties in Delhi

Grievance Status for registration number :
DARPG/E/2017/13169

GRIEVANCE CONCERNS TO

Name Of Complainant	Suraj Parkash Manchanda
Date of Receipt	13/01/2016
Received By Ministry/Department	NCT of Delhi

Grievance Description

A circle rate is the minimum rate for valuation of a plot, independent house, or flat in a particular area or locality. The circle rate differs for various categories of colonies. The circle rates for sale and purchase of properties in a particular area are finalized considering the available infrastructure and other parameters. Presently, there are eight categories of residential colonies in Delhi – A, B, C, D, E, F, G, and H. The circle rates vary depending on the category of a colony or residential area. The Delhi government charges stamp duty for registering a residential property based on the prevailing circle rates of that colony or area. Usually, the properties in Delhi are registered at the circle rates. Therefore, the stamp duty and registration fee, which is calculated as a percentage of the registered price of a property, will vary according to circle rates in the area where the property is situated. Delhi government notifies circle rates in different areas for the purpose of charging stamp duty and registration charges on sale-purchase of properties. The reason for the notification for a specific circle rate in a given area is to simplify the assessment of stamp duty and bring in transparency and efficiency in the property registration process in Delhi and to earn additional revenue.

The circle rates were first introduced in Delhi in 2007, dividing the capital into eight categories, and were notified under the provisions of the Delhi Stamp (Prevention of Undervaluation of Instruments) Rules, 2007 on July 18, 2007. The circle rates in the city was last revised in September 2014. Present circle rate in Delhi of residential land in A category of location like Vasant Vihar, New Delhi is Rs.7,74,000/- per square meter and that of H category like Narela, Delhi is only Rs.23280/- per square meter. It is to be noted that circle rate of land in A category of location is 33 times (3300% more) higher than circle rate of land in H category. However, as per government notification, circle rate of similar area built-up flats is same throughout Delhi whether the flat is located in any of the categories A to H. As per notification dated 22 Sept. 2014, circle rate of LIG flat measuring 30-50 square meter for residential use is only Rs.50,400/- per square meter and that of flat measuring over 100 square meter is Rs.76200/- per square meter throughout Delhi/New Delhi. It means to say that market rate of flat of same size is same across Delhi irrespective of location. If market rate of LIG flat measuring 40 sq. meters in G and H categories is Rs.15 lacs, the same should be available at Rs.15 lacs in A to F categories of location also. The fact is that market value of the same LIG flat is about Rs.1 crore in A, B or C category location, more than 6 times of value of same flat in H category. However the circle rate of LIG flat measuring 40 sq. meter is Rs.37 lacs in all areas. As such, the same area LIG flat at Narela is registered and charged stamp duty at circle rate Rs.37 lacs where the market price is Rs.15 lacs only and the buyer is forced to pay 2.5 times more stamp duty. The result is there are no buyers of flats in Narela and the government is losing revenue. On the other hand the buyer who purchases same area LIG flat in higher A, B or C category location gets registration done by paying stamp duty on circle rate Rs.37 lacs only as notified by the government, although market price of the same flat is about Rs.1 crore. This leads to generation and circulation of black money in real estate transactions and corruption in society. Due to low circle rates of flats in such higher categories, the government is also losing substantial revenue on account of stamp duty and registration charges. The circle rates should be calculated/revised scientifically and be brought near market rate of the property in that area/category of location to curb corruption and raise stamp duty.

Current Status	Case closed
Date of Action	25/07/2017
Remarks	

The matter is under submission for taking decision by Competent Authority regarding for the Circle Rate fixation.

OFFICER CONCERNS TO

Officer Name	**Smt. Manisha Saxena**
Officer Designation	Secretary Revenue
Contact Address	5, Sham Nath Marg, Delhi
Email Address	divcom@nic.in
Contact Number	23962825

Fixing MRP and ceiling price for cardiac stents

Grievance Status for registration number: DARPG/E/2016/02281

GRIEVANCE CONCERNS TO

Name Of Complainant   S P Manchanda

Date of Receipt   13/02/2016

Received By Ministry/Department

Department of Administrative
Reforms and Public Grievances

Grievance Description

CARDIAC STENT is a mesh like tube of thin wire made of stainless steel or cobalt chromium alloy with or without any drug coating. The Stents are used to treat Coronary Atherosclerotic Heart Disease (CAD) and during surgery are implanted in the narrowed/weakened coronary artery; remain inside the body throughout the life, to prevent the artery from closing. They are life saving medical devices so their quality is of utmost importance. Govt. of India, Ministry of Health Family Welfare has notified 14 Medical Devices including Cardiac Stents BMS and DES besides 8 other products as 'DRUGS' under Section 3 (b)(iv) of Drugs Cosmetics Act, 1940, which are regulated. Import of drugs including Medical Devices is controlled by Drugs Controller General India. For import of drug, Registration Certificate in Form 41 (i.e. medical site and products are to be registered) and Import Licence in Form 10 from DCGI, are necessary. Manufacture, sale and distribution are regulated by State Drugs Controllers by licence. Pricing of drugs mentioned in First Schedule of

Drugs (Price) Control Order-2013 (DPCO 2013), is regulated/ fixed by National Pharmaceutical Pricing Authority (NPPA), Department of Pharmaceuticals, Ministry of Chemicals Fertilizers, Government of India. Medical Devices including Stents are non-scheduled drugs. Non-scheduled drugs are not price controlled and their prices are fixed by importer/manufacturers, i.e. such drugs have no control on profit margin. However, their price movement has to be monitored by NPPA on the basis of price list submitted by the importer/manufacturers, in Form V, Schedule II to the DPCO 2013 and their price are not allowed to increase more than 10% in a year. However, Central Government under paragraph 19 of DPCO 2013 has powers to fix MRP of any drug including Stents, under certain circumstances. The Government has so far not utilized their powers to fix MRP of Stents. Over the past couple of years, many patients' organizations, print media as well as government departments have raised concern over the high price of the imported stents, in absence of regulation and patients are forced to pay more than four times of the landed cost. Following a Public Interest Litigation (PIL) filed by Shri Birender Sangwan versus Union of India through Ministry of Health Family Welfare and NPPA vide WP/C 1772/2015 seeking direction of the Court for inclusion of cardiac stents under Price Control, the Hon'ble High Court directed the respondent government on 25.02.2015 to pass an appropriate order to monitor prices of stents in the market within a period of 3 months. Following a complaint from an NGO, FDA Maharashtra made enquiry at importing company which revealed that MRP of the Stents is inflated by 300-1200% to the actual import cost to the company. Due to high MRP, importing company, distributors and hospitals are earning hefty profits, forcing the patients to pay high price for stents. FDA Maharashtra vide their letter dated 18.05.2015, recommended to the NPPA to bring stents under price control. They made such recommendation to NPPA in 2013 also. Para 19 of DPCO, 2013 empowers the Government to fix MRP of any drug including cardiac stents under certain circumstances. The requirements of para 19 are fully met in the case of Stents. The highly exploitive pricing of imported stents makes it out of reach of majority of patients, which constitutes the extraordinary circumstances, in public interest, for proposed intervention under para 19; and therefore, it becomes necessary to regulate the current irrational margin allowed to the importing company, distributors and hospitals and promotional costs incurred and finally in the light of the fact that stents are not currently in the NLEM/First Schedule to DPCO 2013 for purpose of price control, it becomes imperative to regulate the prices of stents under para 19 of the DPCO 2013. Urgent action is required in larger public interest.

Current Status   Case closed
Date of Action   11/04/2016
Remarks

CDSCO deals with safety, quality and efficacy of drugs and pharmaceuticals including cosmetics and medical devices, grievance matter does not come under the purview of CDSCO. However, the grievance matter has been forwarded to National Pharmaceutical Pricing Authority for taking necessary action.

OFFICER CONCERNS TO

Officer Name	**Drug Controller General India**
Officer Designation	DCGI
Contact Address	FDA Bhavan Kotla Road
	New Delhi
Email & contact no.	dcgi@nb.nic.in, 01123236965

Delhi Police not taking action against quack-doctors

CPGRAMS New
Centralized Public Grievance Redress And Monitoring System

Grievance Status for registration number:

DARPG/E2016/ 01134

GRIEVANCE CONCERNS TO

Name Of Complainant	S P Manchanda
Date of Receipt	23/01/2016

Received By Ministry/Department Department of Administrative Reforms and Public Grievances

Grievance Description

This refers to public grievance against Delhi Police not taking action against quacks (doctors with fake degrees) putting the lives of unsuspecting patients at risk. It is despite that fact that more than 400 complaints have been made by the Delhi Medical Council, a regulatory body for registered doctors and medical education in the state. In about 300 cases, however, police have not even lodged first information reports (FIRs). As per Delhi Medical Council officials, there are more than thousands of quacks in Delhi but due to lax attitude of law enforcement agency and no examples of stringent punishment against quacks, there has been steady rise in the number of quacks practicing as qualified doctors in the Capital. Even after the Delhi High Court had instructed the city police to keep track of the large number of fake doctors operating from various parts of the Capital, the police seem to have turned a blind eye to the issue. Among the many guidelines, the high court had stated that at least one raid should be conducted in each of the 11 districts in Delhi every month. The Delhi Police is not even working honestly on this court order.

Current Status   Case closed

Date of Action   15/03/2016

Remarks

Complaint/Representation/Suggestion forward to Delhi Police for appropriate action. It is requested that action taken report may be informed to the petitioner directly.

GRIEVANCE CONCERNS TO

Officer Name   **Shri Govind Mohan**

Officer Designation   Addl. Secretary

Email Address   jsut@nic.in

Contact Number   01123092440

***

Delhi drugs department needs proper regulation

CPGRAMS New
Centralized Public Grievance Redress And Monitoring System

Grievance Status for registration number: GNCTD/E/2017/04557

GRIEVANCE CONCERNS TO

Name Of Complainant   S P Manchanda

Date of Receipt   14/07/2017

Received By Ministry/Department NCT of Delhi

Grievance Description

Delhi drugs department seems to spiral out of control. The department is not headed by a full time qualified Drugs Controller.

The post of Drugs Controller has not been filled-up as per prescribed qualifications in the Recruitment Rules on regular basis for more than 10 years despite court's order and therefore regulatory system is inadequate and weak. As per information received under RTI Act, 2 sanctioned post of Deputy Drug Controller are lying vacant for many years, 14 posts of Drugs Inspectors out of 31 sanctioned posts are also vacant, and there are no Assistant Programmer and Lab Assistant in the department for the last many years. Although the department has laid down norms for number of inspections of licensed premises and number of legal samples collection for testing per month by the Drugs Inspectors but figure of legal samples tested is even less than one sample a day. Besides acute shortage of Drugs Inspectors, the laboratory is considered having inadequate and unsatisfactory infrastructure. The laboratory has no facility for testing drugs under the Schedule C C-1 and no action/steps taken by the government in this regard. The Govt of NCT of Delhi and the Drugs Control Department must provide assurance to the consumers that they will receive only good quality of medicines, at affordable price.

Current Status	Case closed
Date of Action	20/09/2016
Remarks	

It is here by informed that filling up of various vacant posts is a policy matter. However, the department is already in a process of filling the vacant posts of Drugs Inspectors in consultation with UPSC. Regarding Drugs Testing Laboratories, Government of NCT of Delhi, and the Department has already signed a MOU with Government of India, Ministry Health Family Welfare, for strengthening and Up gradation of Drugs Testing Laboratories so as to meet the international standards.

OFFICER CONCERNS TO

Officer Name	**A K Nasa**
Officer Designation	Deputy Drugs Controller
Contact Address	F–17, Karkardooma,
	4th Floor, Shahadara, Delhi
Email Address	dirdcd@nic.in
Contact Number	22393701

****

Medical devices sold at inflated prices (MRP) in hospitals

CPGRAMS New
Centralized Public Grievance Redress And Monitoring System

Grievance Status for registration number:

DPHAM/E/2017/00078

GRIEVANCE CONCERNS TO

Name Of Complainant	S P Manchanda
Date of Receipt	15/03/2017
Received By Ministry/Department	Pharmaceutical

Grievance Description

After cardiac stents, there are about 14 more medical devices e.g. catheters, orthopedic implants, intra-ocular lenses, IV cannulae, bone cements, heart valves, disposable syringes, needles, internal prosthetic implants that are rampantly being sold to hapless patients at inflated prices (MRP) in the hospitals and nursing homes in India. In terms of steep retail markups, orthopedic implants come closest to cardiac stents. It is common knowledge that imported hip and knee implants see profit margins in the range of 500 to 1000 percent whereas Indian implants are sold at margins of 200-500 percent. The cost of intra-ocular lenses varies widely depending upon the profit margin of the hospitals and surgeons. Consumables are not just sold at arbitrarily inflated MRPs, but also billed in bulk to make extra money. Although some of the medical devices are classified as 'drugs' under Section 3 of the Drugs and Cosmetics Act, none feature in the list of essential medicines, as a result their prices have not been capped by NPPA and NPPA merely ensures that their (arbitrarily fixed) MRP is not increased by more than 10 percent as per rules. It is therefore important to curb the extent of profiteering in these medical devices and add them to the list of essential medicines before their prices (MRPs) can be capped/regulated by NPPA. It is significant here to note that when an original manufacturer sells a medical device, the cost of innovation, packaging and everything else is built into it. Further, the importer spends nothing on R and D or packaging. Their money is only spent on marketing, commissions and distorting the price-system. With price-capping, afford-ability will increase. Union Health Ministry is therefore requested to add these medical devices (just like cardiac stents) to the list of essential medicines to enable NPPA to cap their prices to curb 'loot' by the companies, distributors and the hospitals or surgeons in order to help the helpless patients in larger public interest.

Current Status	Case closed
Date of Action	02/09/2017
Remarks	

The suggestions have been noted. Thank you for valuable suggestion.

OFFICER CONCERNS TO

Officer Name	**Devendra Kumar**
Officer Designation	Director
Email Address	devendra.kumar08@nic.in
Contact Number	01123324930

***

Eye banking system in India needs support to prevent corneal blindness

CPGRAMS New

Centralized Public Grievance Redress And Monitoring System

Current Status	Case closed
Date of Action	11/10/2019

Received By Ministry/Department Prime Ministers Office

Grievance Description

भारत एक युवा देश है अर्थात् भारत की 65% जनसंख्या 35 वर्ष से कम आयु की है। युवाओं की नई सोच, उनकी ऊर्जा, समाज के लिए कुछ कर गुजरने का जज्बा ही उन्हें युवा बनाता है। भारत में प्रतिवर्ष पाँच लाख लोग अंगों की कमी के कारण मृत्यु को प्राप्त होते हैं जबकि एक वर्ष में मरने वालों की संख्या लगभग आठ लाख है। हमारे देश में 80 लाख लोग ऐसे हैं जिन्हें अगर कोर्निया प्राप्त हो जाए तो वे दुनिया को देख सकेंगे। अगर सभी मरणोपरांत आँखों के दान का निश्चय कर लें तो भारत केवल 10 दिनों में कोर्निया की अंधता को समाप्त कर सकता है। अगर अंग दान एक आंदोलन बनता है तो संभवत: भारत अंगों की उपलब्धता कराने में पूरे विश्व में एक अग्रणी भूमिका निभा सकता है।

इसके लिए युवाओं की भूमिका बहुत महत्त्वपूर्ण है। बोन मैरो वस्टे मसैल दान 18 से 35 वर्ष की आयु का कोई भी युवा कर सकता है। इससे Blood Cancer व बहुत सी ला इलाज बीमारियों का इलाज संभव है। इसके लिए खून की जाँच के माध्यम से HLA टाइप को पूरे विश्वस्तर पर बन रही एक सूचि में दाखिल कर लिया जाता है।

     Embrace Your Own Power to Fight Corruption

HLA टाइप के परिवार में मिलान होने का अनुपात 2.5% है पर परिवार के बाहर इस मिलान का अनुपात 10,000 में से एक का है। अब बोन मैरो का दान पहले की तरह मुश्किल व कष्टप्रद नहीं है। अब केवल 3–4 घंटे में दान करने वाला व्यक्ति सकुशल घर आ सकता है। बोन मैरो में रक्त बनाने की क्षमता होती है। इसके प्रत्यारोपण से कैंसर का ईलाज संभव है। सटेम सैल जीवन की प्राथमिक इकाई है, इससे श्ारीर के किसी भी अंग को नया जीवन दिया जा सकता है। इस विजय को आगे बढ़ाने के लिए युवाओं की व युवाओं के द्वारा जागरूकता की एक महत्त्वपूर्ण भूमिका है। विश्ोज़ तौर पर मैडिकल के छात्रों व डॉक्टरों को आगे आना चाहिए।

हमारे देश्ा में HLA रजिस्ट्री अधिक विस्तृत हो सके इसके लिए भारत सरकार को सभी राज्य स्तरों पर पर्याप्त व्यवस्थाएँ करनी चाहिए ताकि प्रधानमंत्री श्री नरेंद्र मोदी के सपनों का भारत अधिक स्वस्थ व सबल बन सके।

Remarks

Sir, this is to inform you that the eye banking system in India is being further strengthened to control preventable corneal blindness by providing better education on eye care for general public specially farmers and industrial workers (to avoid eye injuries at work), provision for better training of medical personnel to take care of corneal injuries and infections promptly under the National Programme for Control of Blindness & Visual Impairment (NPCBVI), better training of ophthalmologist for quality cataract surgeries so that post-operative corneal complication is minimal, making mandatory notification of deaths (MDN) by all departments in major hospitals to the eye bank personnel to timely counselling and removal of donated eyes etc.

GRIEVANCE CONCERNS TO

Officer Name	**Shri Rajeev Attri**
Officer Designation	Under Secretary
Email Address	r.attri54@nic.in
Contact Number	01123061883

***

Poor awareness programs of food adulteration

CPGRAMS New
Centralized Public Grievance Redress And Monitoring System

Grievance Status for registration number : PMOPG/E/2019/0697898

GRIEVANCE CONCERNS TO

Name Of Complainant   Suraj Parkash Manchanda

Date of Receipt   05/12/2019

Received By Ministry/Department Prime Ministers Office

Grievance Description

This grievance is in the context of the poor awareness programs being run by the government on raising the problem of food products adulteration and to prevent fatal diseases like cancer due to these contamination, and also demands the government to increase the health budget. The government has enacted strong laws against adulteration at the central and state levels. But due to corruption/ lack of will power by the enforcing agencies and poor awareness in public, the situation is getting worse. All daily household items are being adulterated. Adulteration is present in everything from milk we used in the morning to food eaten at night. Daily life food have been found to be highly toxic and carcinogenic. Variety of chemical like, adulteration of detergent and urea in milk, harmful wax layer on fruits, malachite green dye on green vegetables, use of oxytocin to increase the size of vegetables, calcium carbide for quick ripening, metanil yellow in pulses/turmeric which may damage nervous system, eckhart fungus in wheat and much more materials that are being sold in the market with adulteration

    Embrace Your Own Power to Fight Corruption

without any legal objection. Rampant use of pesticides, insecticides prevention of corps and seeds along with use of irrigation water that is high in arsenic content, contamination starts from farm level itself.Children under 5 years of age carry about 40 percent of food water borne disease burden in India. Diarrhea (6514 deaths), hepatitis (2143), typhoid (2061), cholera (20) these are killer food and water borne disease that are growing in our country due to lack of awareness. World Health Organisation (WHO) estimates suggest that nearly 22 percent of all infection related deaths are water and food borne. About 70 percent of deaths are likely to be of food-borne origin. According to the NSS 71st round survey and IHME, Food contamination is a huge economic burden and estimated total direct medical cost due to food-borne water-borne disease are 32,941 crores rupees in 2016-17, and could reach 7,37,457 crores by 2022. According to data from the National Health Profile in (NCHP) 2019, general cancer cases including oral cancer, cervical cancer, breast cancer cases have increased by about 324 percent across the country. After 5 years we will have more cancer-hospitals than general-hospitals in the country. On the one hand, adulterated foods are increasing in the country and on the other hand, according to NHP, the condition of medical services sector in India is quite pathetic and miserable. Government should develop an awareness system related to food/water spoilage and contamination. Quality control and laboratory testing in the unorganized sector, food hygiene should also be compiled with inspection process of food establishment, also may assign research team for identifiable symptoms of food and water borne diseases. Keeping these recommendations in mind, the government should spread awareness about harm caused by alcohol, smoking and adulteration in public. Strict law is mandatory against adulteration.

Strictness in the law and awareness in the public can only stop the adulteration completely. It is also necessary to consider the subject of increasing the health budget. The central government should spend 2.5 percent of GDP on health while states should spend 8 percent of the state GDP on health from 4.7 percent on average. Central government should immediately pay serious attention to this problem and make guidelines accordingly to save our future generations from menace of adulteration in India.

Current Status	Case closed
Date of Action	09/12/2019
Remarks	

Sir, your observations have been noted. Thanks

GRIEVANCE CONCERNS TO

Officer Name	**Sh. Ashish V Gawai,** Deputy Secretary
Email & contact no.	av.gawai@nic.in, 23062292

Pathetic condition of North MCD Gym needs care

Grievance Status

Grievance No	2017070273
Date of Grievance	01/09/2017
Complainant Name	S. P. Manchanda
Contact Nos.	(Landline),9891827669(Mobile)
Category	Online Entryby Citizen
Complainant Address	C-2/35B, Keshav Puram, Delhi 110035
E–MailID	suraj_1511@yahoo.com

Grievance Details

The Gym situated at first floor of Community Hall opposite C-2 block Keshav Puram Delhi is in a pathetic state as for the last month there is no electricity. The care-taker of the Gym is careless towards its cleanliness and maintenance of equipments which are now in very bad shape. MCD has spent lakhs of rupees for the welfare of people living in Keshav Puram area but the residents are not able to take advantage of facility provided by the government due to lethargy of staff deputed for the maintenance and cleanliness of Gym. The staff do not care our requests for improvement. Please do the needful immediately so that the residents of this area use this Gym for which government has spent a lot.

Grievance Site Address:	Community Hall, C-2 block, Keshav Puram, Delhi
Department	MCD NORTH
Action Taken	08/01/2019

The estimate has been passed for works of electrical and for sanitation a safaikaramchari has already been deployed there. As far as repairingof equipment of Gym the department will take estimate about the repairing of equipment of Gym from contractor. As well as maintenance works already in progress.

Contact Details	**MR. ASHOK KUMAR,**
	ACO CSD,
	ddcsdmcd@gmail.com
	9968096810

***

Delhi needs CNG/Electric cremation to curb pollution

Grievance Status

Grievance No	2018030793
Date of Grievance	22/03/2018
Complainant Name	S.P. Manchanda
Contact Nos.	(Landline),9891827669(Mobile)
Category	Online Entryby Citizen::
Complainant Address	C-2/35B,
	Keshav Puram,Delhi110035
E-Mail ID	suraj_1511@yahoo.com

Grievance Details

Cremating a human corpse by traditional method requires 300 - 400 Kg of wood. Every day hundreds of dead bodies are cremated by using wood in our city Delhi, which not only deplete green cover of the earth but also produce tons of poisonous smoke polluting our environment with carbon dioxide, carbon monoxide and many other noxious gases. These gases are extremely harmful to our health and can cause many incurable diseases such as asthma, T.B. and cancer etc. Elderly People Forum believes that over consumption of wood is one of the major cause for the destruction of our ecosystem. Therefore our Forum is making every possible effort to educate people not to cremate dead bodies by using wood. But the Delhi government has installed only 3 CNG/electric cremation machines in Delhi. Govt should create awareness about the ill effect of burning wood for cremating dead bodies and about its negative impact on environment. We advise everyone to use CNG or Electric Cremation System because It is hygienic. It is environment friendly. It reduces a body to powdery ash. It is cost-effective. Religious prayers, vedas, mantras and traditional rituals can still be performed while cremating a dead body by CNG or electric cremation system. Many NGO's are working in India that are trying to reduce pollution due to cremation sector, as a result of development they developed a system called MGCS (Mokshda Green Cremation System). The main objectives of this project is to decrease the use of wood from 70% to 75%, which may lead to reduce the carbon dioxide coming out. Saving of wood also reduces cremation cost substantially & makes MGCS affordable to people below poverty line. We urge all socially conscious people to promote CNG / Electric / MGCS Cremation System for cremating dead bodies to save our environment and request the Delhi government to arrange installation of latest cremation machines in each district of the NCT of Delhi. Regards, President - Elderly People Forum, Keshav Puram.

Grievance Site Address: C 2/35 B, Keshav Puram, Delhi 110035

Department	MCD EAST
Action Taken	11/12/2018

The Public Health Dept., EDMC is making all concerted efforts to minimise the utility of wood based conventional cremation system. Projects for establishing wood based pollution free cremation system has been taken up by establishing atleast one such unit in Ghazipur, Jwala Nagar, Karkardooma and Seemapuri Cremation grounds. Secondly, one CNG based cremation unit is also being taken up for establishing eco friendly cremation system at Ghazipur Cremation Ground.

Contact Details

Dr. Somshekhar, Addl.

Municipal Health Officer

011-66667300,

addlmhoedmc@gmail.com

MCD authorities not paying attention to a large size plot/park misused by miscreants for keeping their animals

Grievance Status

Grievance No	2018083588
Date of Grievance	24/07/2018
Complainant Name	S.P. Manchanda
Contact Nos.	(Landline),9891827669(Mobile)
Category	Online Entry by Citizen
Complainant Address	Block C 2, Flat No.35 B Keshav Puram, Delhi 110035
E-Mail ID	suraj_1511@yahoo.com

Grievance Details

This is my grievance against the North MCD authorities not paying attention to a large size plot/park called Swaran Jayanti Park opposite C-2 block Keshav Puram, Delhi 110035. This big-size plot is abandoned / not in use since last more than 10 years and is therefore misused by miscreants for keeping their animals and others/drinkers consuming liquor in the park without any action by the police or MCD authorities. RWA Lawrence Road C-2 block Keshavpuram demands strict action against those who take their animals inside this park for roaming and feeding, thus making it polluted and dirty place to walk. Further we request the MCD authorities to replace the large-size gate to a small gate which will prevent entry of cows and buffaloes inside the park. It would be better if the North MCD allots this plot to RWA

Lawrence Road C-2 pocket, for parking vehicles of their residents because most of residents park their cars/bikes on the side of main road near this plot and there is always risk of accidents and theft of their vehicles. The C-2 block residents have more than 300 cars and the colony can accommodate only 100 cars inside the gates, rest 200 cars have to be parked outside the colony. Please consider our proposal for parking space in this adjoining park opposite C-2 block in larger public interest.

Grievance Site Address: Block C2, Flat No. 35 B

Keshav Puram, Delhi110035

Department MCD NORTH

Action Taken 12/09/2018

10 Dairy owners have been prosecuted on dated 16.07.2018 to 19.08.2018 and will be continuing in future also.

Contact Details

Dr. Jaibir Singh Dagar,

Dy.Director(VS)

 Embrace Your Own Power to Fight Corruption

Unauthorized construction of shops facing road between Gurudwara and Mandir

Grievance Status

Grievance No	2019007426
Date of Grievance	20/01/2019
Complainant Name	S.P. Manchanda
Contact Nos.	(Land Line),9891827669(Mobile)
Category	Online Entryby Citizen::
Complainant Address	Recreation Centre, C-2/35B, Keshav Puram,Delhi110035
E-Mail ID	suraj_1511@yahoo.com

Grievance Details

We are aggrieved due to unauthorised and illegal construction of shops facing the road/street between Gurdwara Sri-Guru-Singh-Sabha and Pardeshwar Dham Mandir C-3 block Keshav Puram, Delhi-110035. Because of these shops between the Gurudwara and the Mandir, the street has become narrow and also responsible for pollution due to activity of a noodle-shop there. The shopkeepers have also constructed stairs facing the street in front of their shops further adding difficulty for the pedestrians and passing vehicles. Some people are also doing contrcution activity nearby and have thrown malba on the road further causing pollution for the public passing through this road/street. The authorities should immediately take suitable action for removing unauthorised construction and malba, thus giving relief to people and help us to curb pollution in the area.

Grievance Site Address: Recreation Centre,
C-4block, Keshav Puram,Delhi

Department   MCDNORTH

Action Taken   29/01/2019

Matter of unauthorized construction is related to Building Department/KPZ 2. The matter of unauthorized Noodle shop is related to Licensing Department as well as Health Department Keshav Puram Zone. As regard, encroachment the action shall be taken as per policy/guidelines after carried out detailed inspection of the area under reference.

Contact Details   **Sh. K.K. Sharma,**
Executive Engineer M II
01127305387,
eemiikpz@gmail.com

Broken windows of Varishth Nagrik Manoranjan Kendra

Grievance Status

Grievance No	2018080155
Date of Grievance	17/07/2018
Complainant Name	S.P. Manchanda
Contact Nos.	(Landline),9891827669(Mobile)
Category	Online Entry by Citizen::
Complainant Address	C-2/35B, Keshav Puram, Delhi110035
E-Mail ID	suraj_1511@yahoo.com

Grievance Details

This refers to senior citizens' grievance against the North MCD authorities for not attending the request of repairing window panes of Varishth Nagrik Manoranjan Kendra (Senior Citizen Recreation Center) at C-4 block Keshav Puram, Delhi. It is now rainy season and the elderly people who go there for recreation face much difficulty when rain-water enters the hall and rooms of the Center through broken windows and makes elderly people difficult to sit and walk there. After the rains, they have to put much labour to throw out dirty water gathered inside. Further there is danger of diseases due to accumulation of dirty rain-water inside the building. The competent authority should look into the matter sympathetically and arrange to repair/replace the broken windows immediately. Thanks and regards.

Grievance Site Address: Block C 2, Flat No. 35 B Keshav Puram

Department	MCDNORTH
Action Taken	19/11/2018

In this matter it is submitted that the Community Services Department has already been sent a letter to Engg. Deptt. (maintenance-I) and the matter is under process and will be done soon.

Contact Details	**MR. ASHOK KUMAR,**
	ACO CSD
	ddcsdmcd@gmail.com,
	968096810

***

Only two Old-age homes in the capital city of Delhi

Grievance Status

Grievance No	201686304
Date of Grievance	07/09/2016
Complainant Name	S.P. Manchanda
Contact Nos.	(Landline),9891827669(Mobile)
Category	Online Entry by Citizen ::
Complainant Address	Deenbandhu Chottu Ram Dispensary, C-2/35 B, Keshav Puram, Delhi 110035
E-Mail ID	suraj_1511@yahoo.com

 Embrace Your Own Power to Fight Corruption

Grievance Details

Many older people in Delhi, in the capital of India, face problems like poor health, hunger and lack of shelter. A monthly old age pension is the only support the poor elderly people receive from the government. Nowadays it is very difficult to stay together as a family because many young people migrate to cities or abroad in search of better opportunities. This situation makes older persons look for old age homes. But there are only two governmental elderly homes in whole Delhi, one at Lampur with capacity of 100 persons and another at Bindapur with capacity of only 50 persons; and they are also in poor condition. The Government of NCT of Delhi should look into grievance of elderly persons and stand up for the interests and rights of older people. The competent authority need to take the main role in improving the present pathetic situation. We humbly request the government authorities to come up with new policies and programs in cooperation with international and national organizations working for older people.

Grievance Site Address:	C 2 - 35 B, Keshav Puram, Delhi 110035
Department	SOCIAL WELFARE
Action Taken	15/09/2016

This is in reference to your PGMS Greivance ID no. 201686304 on the subject cited above. In this regard, it is to inform you that the Department of Social welfare, GNCT of Delhi has intitated construction of 10 more Old age homes in different areas of Delhi i.e. at Chitranjan Park, Rohini, Kanti Nagar, Paschim Vihar, geeta colony, Wazirpur and Chattarpur, Janakpuri, Sarita Vihar and Vasant Kunj to cater the needs and requirement of Old Age homes.

Contact Details

Neelam Venkatachalam,
Dy Director (SS)
23713603
ddss.dsw@gmail.com

***

Govt dispensary not issuing the medicines to pensioners beneficiaries

Grievance Status

Grievance No	201669451
Date of Grievance	16/07/2016
Complainant Name	S.P. Manchanda
Contact Nos.	(Landline),9891827669 (Mobile)
Category	Online Entry by Citizen
Complainant Address	Deenbandhu Chottu Ram Dispensary, C-2/35 B, Keshav Puram, Delhi 110035
E-Mail ID	suraj_1511@yahoo.com

Grievance Details

I regret to point out that Keshav Puram Dispensary, under Delhi Government, has not been issuing to the pensioners beneficiaries, the medicines prescribed by the empanelled hospitals where they are getting treatment, for past more than four months, for the reason that the supplier empanelled chemist, M/s Shikha Medicos (Prop. Sanyog Enterprises Pvt. Ltd., KD Block, Pitampura, Delhi-110034 has stopped supplying the medicines. However, other empanelled chemists have been regularly been supplying medicines to the dispensaries allotted to them and pensioners have been getting all the prescribed medicines from all such dispensaries. This is great injustice to the pensioners beneficiaries covered under the Keshav Puram Dispensary. It is to be noted that Pensioner Beneficiaries, under DGEHS, are entitled for supply of all the medicines prescribed by the empaneled hospitals , by the Delhi Govt. dispensaries, as per SPO (DGEHS), DHS, Govt. of NCT of Delhi's letter No. F. 25(iii)/DGEHS/DHS/359/2013-14/25231-448 dated 12.05.2014. Doctors working at B4 Keshav Puram Dispensary ask the patients to buy such prescribed the medicines from local chemists and claim the amounts from their department/ministry. The doctors show helplessness saying that all medicines are not provided by the department nor made available when requisitioned. The Dispensary has not taken positive sincere steps with the authorities, for making alternate arrangements, for supply of prescribed medicines to the pensioner beneficiaries. Not providing prescribed medicines by the Keshav Puram Dispensary and others, is a great injustice to the pensioner beneficiaries of the area covered under above allotted empanelled chemist. The pensioners have been facing great difficulties and hardships in buying/procuring medicines from the market and then submitting bills to their Department, for reimbursement which also takes long time for clearance by their departments. Competent authorities should take suitable action.

Grievance Site Address:	Deenbandhu Chottu Ram Dispensary, Keshav Puram, Delhi 110035
Department	Director Health Services
Action Taken	05/08/2016

The medicines supply through the ALCs has been restored from 01/08/2016. Beneficiary may visit the attached dispensary for the medicines prescribed by empanelled hospital.

Contact Details

Dr. Deepak Kumar Singh,
Addl. Director (DGEHS),
sopdgehs@gmail.com,
22391435

***

Committee after committee but no decision to rationalize circle rates in Delhi to curb corruption

Grievance Status

Grievance No	2016104707
Date of Grievance	09/11/2016
Complainant Name	S P Manchanda
Contact Nos.	(LandLine),9891827669(Mobile)
Category	Online Entry by Citizen
Complainant Address	President, Elderly People Forum, C 2 / 35 B, Keshav Puram, Delhi 110035
E-Mail ID	suraj_1511@yahoo.com

Grievance Details

An 'empowered committee' has been constituted by the Delhi government to review discrepancies in the circle rates in certain areas of the national capital. According to information received under RTI Act, the Revenue Department has sought public suggestions on the review of circle rates by 16 August 2016. The Department has decided to review circle rates for charging stamp duty and registration charges for a property. It published advertisement in leading newspapers after it received several complaints against the existing rates. After receiving suggestions and grievances, the empowered committee will submit the recommendations to the Delhi government, and circle rates will be revised accordingly. It is worthy to mention here that an expert committee was constituted in 2014 too and the said committee submitted its report in March 2014 to the government. The report revealed that existing circle rates in Delhi are illogical, irrational and arbitrarily fixed. The Committee recommended for increasing the categories of location and rationalising the circle rates to curb corruption and raise revenue. Honourable High Court of Delhi vide its Order dated 23.12.2015 also suggested revision of rates and to register property below circle rates in areas where circle rates are higher than prevailing market rates. But as per information received under RTI Act, the Revenue Department has not yet taken any view on High Court Order. On the contrary the Revenue Department spent lakhs of rupees on advertisements inviting suggestions and grievances from general public and constituted an empowered committee once again to revise circle rates. It is public grievance that committee has not yet started functioning even after 3 months of receiving complaints and suggestions The Honourable CM and Dy. CM should look into this matter urgently and issue suitable order to the committee members to send recommendations to the government.

Grievance Site Address:	President, Elderly People Forum, C 2/35 B, Keshav Puram, Delhi -35
Department	Revenue Department
Action Taken	31/07/2019

The matter i.e fixation of circle rates is a policy matter and decision will soon be taken by the competent authorities.

Contact Details	**Sh. Nitin Jindal, SDM (HQ) VI** 23965184, sdmhq4divcomm.delhi@nic.in

Inconvenience due to broken footpath

Grievance Status

Grievance No	201680933
Date of Grievance	22/08/2016
Complainant Name	S.P. Manchanda
Contact Nos.	(LandLine),9891827669(Mobile)
Category	Online Entry by Citizen ::
Complainant Address	C-2/35 B, Keshav Puram, Delhi - 110035
E-Mail ID	suraj_1511@yahoo.com

Grievance Details

This refers to sanction of funds for resurfacing of footpath of central park at C-2 block Keshav Puram North-West Delhi, the work commenced in the last week of March 2016. Though the whole footpath was dug-up promptly, there are no signs of repair being undertaken. This has caused great inconvenience to the residents as they have not been able to use and enjoy the park facilities for over four months. The delay in question has been repeatedly brought to the notice of authorities/engineers concerned but there has been no progress whatsoever. We request the concerned engineers/ authorities to solve our grievance urgently so that footpath is repaired on priority basis and the residents, particularly the elderly people of this pocket, can use this park in the morning and evening times.

 Embrace Your Own Power to Fight Corruption

Grievance Site Address	C-2/35 B, Keshav Puram,
	Delhi – 110035
Department	MCD NORTH
Action Taken	26/08/2016

The dressing of walkway of Central Park has been done and for remaining repair, the estimate is under pipeline.

Contact Details

Ms. Ira Singhal,
Deputy Commissioner

***

Non supply of medicines by dispensary to DGEHS pensioners

Grievance Status

Grievance No	201690422
Date of Grievance	21/09/2016
Complainant Name	S P Manchanda
Contact Nos.	(LandLine),9891827669(Mobile)
Category	Online Entry by Citizen ::
Complainant Address	President, Elderly People Forum,
	C 2 - 35 B, Keshav Puram,
	Delhi 110035
E-Mail ID	suraj_1511@yahoo.com

Grievance Details

This refers to my grievance No. 201672756 dated 26.07.2016

regarding non-supply of medicines to pensioners under DGEHS. The grievance was resolved and it was informed that medicines supply through ALC was restored w.e.f. 1.8.2016. It is ironic that on 2.9.2016 Raymedica Pharmaceuticals have written a letter to the Director (DHS), F-17, Karkadooma, Delhi regarding suspension/ stoppage of supplies to DGEHS (NW4) because agreed payment schedule has not been followed by the government (copy of letter attached). The Govt of NCT of Delhi should immediately intervene and settle the issue promptly so that pensioners and senior citizens of Delhi are not troubled/harassed again and again due to non-availability of medicines in the government dispensary.

Grievance Site Address:

President, Elderly People Forum,
C 2 - 35 B, Keshav Puram,
Delhi 110035

Department   Director Health Services

Action Taken   11/11/2016

The beneficiary was contacted telephonically on 10/11/2016 at 4.50 P.M. It was informed that Authorized Local Chemist has already been appointed in North District w.e.f. 21/10/2016. The difficulty regarding not functioning of MIS has also been resolved vide circular dated 07/11/2016. It was further informed that the tender is for 01 year so that the beneficiaries of DGEHS may not suffer at any stage. The complainant was satisfied with the reply.

Contact Details   **Dr. Deepak Kumar Singh,**

Addl. Director (DGEHS)
sopdgehs@gmail.com, 22391435,

Monkey menace is a big problem in many parts of Delhi

Grievance Status

Grievance No	2019047708
Date of Grievance	27/04/2019
Complainant Name	Suraj Parkash Manchanda
Contact Nos.	(LandLine),9891827669(Mobile)
Category	Online Entry by Citizen ::
Complainant Address	Block C-2/ 35 B Keshav Puram, Delhi-35
E-Mail ID	suraj_1511@yahoo.com

Grievance Details

This refers to media report (Navbharat Times, 20/10/18) revealing that MCD has not enough monkey catchers which is a great concern for society. Damage by raiding monkeys has become a menace of unprecedented magnitude. The number of monkeys straying is on the rise. Monkey menace has increased in the recent past in Keshav Puram Delhi. Monkeys often ransack homes and bite people in this residential colony. It is almost impossible for elder citizens and children to step out of their house. There have been many instances that they destroy clothes, plants, pipes, cable wires and constantly disturb local people any day time. As days are passing, they are rising at large. Almost daily cases of monkey bites are found which can cause Rabies and can be fatal. So far, relocating them outside the colony has been a colossal failure.

In fact, monkey menace is big problem in many parts of Delhi. Monkeys have a religious place in the Hindu dominating society. Fighting monkeys is becoming difficult due to opposition from the civil society. But the main problem is, corporations do not have enough monkey catchers in their departments. Sterilization is not so successful, they need translocation. A team of monkey catcher specialist may be helpful. Government should release some article action points and tips covering awareness as to how to fight the increasing monkey menace, may also approach schools to create awareness among children. Some hoardings and notice boards giving tips to fight the monkey menace may also be displayed near the temples and at some important locations. Monkeys fell into the wild life category and govt should keep it away from the public reach. Most importantly, the Govt should arrange enough money catchers and use them judicially.

Grievance Site Address:

Block C 2/35 B Keshav Puram, Delhi-35

Department MCD NORTH

Action Taken 05/06/2019

The monkey contractor has been directed to fix cage for trapping monkeys.

Contact Details

Dr. Jaibir Singh Dagar,

Dy. Director (VS)

Burglary cases happening in Keshav Puram, Delhi

Grievance Status

Grievance No	2018041528
Date of Grievance	16/04/2018
Complainant Name	Suraj Parkash Manchanda
Contact Nos.	(LandLine),9891827669(Mobile)
Category	Online Entry by Citizen ::
Complainant Address	C-2 / 35 B, Keshav Puram, Delhi 110035
E-Mail ID	suraj_1511@yahoo.com

Grievance Details

This refers to frequent burglary cases happening in Keshav Puram area causing serious law and order problem in the DDA colony. It is submitted that from last 6 months, number of cases has shattered the otherwise peaceful area and the atmosphere of fear and uncertainty has demoralized the KeshavPuram residents. Recently in Feb/March 2018, 15-20 car-batteries were stolen/taken out from cars parked in C-4 block. After FIR lodged, a meeting with members of RWA was held in the chairmanship of ACP/AV on 5.3.18 in connection with increasing incidents of theft cases in the area. Despite police assurance of sincere efforts to trace and book the culprits, in next month on 12.4.2018 locks of 9 shops in A-1 market were found broken and shutters damaged and entire cash of shops looted. It is unfortunate that none of the cases is solved which gives encouragement to anti-social elements making them fearless to execute the next crime very soon. As per information received under RTI Act, there is acute shortage of staff at Keshav Puram police-station. Against sanctioned strength of 38 HC and 101 constables, posted strength at PS Keshav Puram is only 19 HC and 51 Constables (just half). Sir, every innocent unfortunate victim here looks towards the police as a ray of ultimate hope. We request the competent authority to employ the adequate staff at the KP police station and serious action should be taken promptly on the theft/burglary cases happened in the area ensuring optimum safety to the residents of this Keshav Puram area.

Grievance Site Address:

	C-2 / 35 B, Keshav Puram,
	Delhi-35
Department	Delhi Police
Action Taken	02/05/2018

The matter has been got enquired through ACP/Ashok Vihar which revealed that the detailes of crime reported in the area of Beat No. 2 of PS Keshav Puram from 01.01.2018 to 20.04.2018 is as under:- As per record on 12.04.2018, on burglary incident reported from the area of Beat No.02 of Ps Keshav Puram. However, one burglary theft incident was reported from A-1 Block, Keshav Puram (Area of beat No. 4). The details of Strategy/Action taken for prevention of crime in the area of beat No. 02 of Keshav Puram is as under:- 1. Area of beat No. 02 of PS Keshav Puram is surrounded by C-4, JJ Cluster Area. Two Constables are deployed near Railway line/JJ Cluster area to keep watch on suspected persons. 2. On 05.03.2018, a Public meeting was held with the resident of C-4, jj Cluster Area. Two constables are deployed near Railway line JJ colony area to keep watch on suspected persons. On 05/03/2018 a public meeting was held with the residents of

C Block Keshav Puram in the Chairman Ship of ACP/Ashok Vihar regarding prevention of theft in the area foot patrolling and group patrolling are doing by SHO/Keshav Puram along with beat staff..meeting with members of Eyes and Ears Rwa members and Prahari is also conducted on regular basis. Place of occurrence date and time of MVT cases theft cases has ben analyzed and supplied to beat staff for taking necessary action. ERV staff qrt staff and Commander 77 has been directed to conducted to make extra efforts for workout the pending cases of MVT and other theft cases. Two police assistance booth have been constructed in this area for proper presence of police personals in the beat area. It is facts there are only 43 males constables are posted against a sactioned strength of 101. There is shortage 58 constables. The above strength is very much much less day to day functions of PS Keshav Puram.

***

LG should intervene to rationalize circle rates in Delhi

Grievance No	2019012103
Date of Grievance	24/10/2019
Complainant Name	Suraj Parkash Manchanda
Contact Nos.	(LandLine),9891827669(Mobile)
Category	Online Entry by Citizen ::
Complainant Address	C-2/35 B, Keshav Puram, Delhi 110035

Grievance Details

Regarding irrational and arbitrarily fixed circle rates in Delhi which have not been revised properly even after 5 years (last revised in Sept. 2014) despite expert committee and empowered committee recommendations in this regard and corruption is still going on unabated in real estate transactions till date. PGMS 2018051589 was responded by the Revenue Department SDM II on 14.6.2018 stating that the matter of circle rates fixation in Delhi is under consideration and decision will SOON be taken by the competent authorities. But decision has not been taken by authorities till date. Action Required. It is requested Delhi govt should promptly take the decision for proper revision of circle rates as per recommendations of committee in larger public interest to curb corruption and involvement of black money in real estate transactions in the capital city of India. BUREAUCRATIC LETHARGY IS THE WORST FORM OF CORRUPTION.

Grievance Site Address:	C-2/35 B, Keshav Puram, Delhi 110035
Department	Revenue Department
Action Taken	18/11/2019 Revision of Circle rate is underway.
Contact Details	

Arun Kumar Jha,

SDM HQ II,

23965184, hqsdm2@nic.in

RIGHT TO INFORMATION ACT, 2005

RTI KILLS CORRUPTION

It is no secret that government functioning in India is characterized by large scale leakage and misappropriation of public funds. In addition to corruption, there are other problems, such as, non-performance of duties and inefficient functioning that plague government departments. In a country where citizens are vigilant and ask information about government activities, they can monitor public works, prevent scams and exert pressure to ensure that public funds are utilized effectively and that government employees perform their duties efficiently and honestly. Listed below are some of the major scams and anomalies exposed by the Right To Information Act (RTI).

Adarsh Society Scam

What was meant to be a six-storey building for the widows of Kargil war heroes, turned into a 31-storey high-rise called Adarsh Housing Society. Located in Mumbai's posh residential area Colaba, it soon became the abode of politicians, bureaucrats, and top military officers. The nexus was exposed by RTI activists Simpreet Singh and Yogacharya Anandji. The expose revealed that the piece of land did not belong to the state government but to the Ministry of Defence and culminated in the resignation of Ashok Chavan, the then chief minister of Maharashtra.

2G Scam

The 2G scam or the telecom sector scandal, which took place in the UPA regime, revolved around the government auctioning the 2G spectrum. Top ministers had allegedly colluded to undercharge certain mobile phone companies while allocating the frequencies, in exchange for a bribe. This reportedly cost the exchequer a whopping Rs 1.76 lakh crore. The massive abuse of power came to light when an RTI was filed by activist Subhash Chandra Agrawal. Several big names were involved in the scam including former Telecom Minister A Raja and DMK leader Kanimozhi.

Commonwealth Games Scam

An RTI filed by a non-profit organization revealed that the Delhi government had diverted Rs 744 crore from funds earmarked for the welfare of the Dalit community to the Commonwealth Games. The non-profit body – Housing and Land Rights Network – also found that most of the diverted funds were expended on amenities that existed only on paper, suggesting further corruption and money laundering.

23,000 loan fraud cases in past 5 years

Replying to an RTI, the Reserve Bank of India (RBI) had informed that 23,000 cases of fraud have been reported by various banks in the past five years, which involved Rs 1 lakh crore.

RTI stands for 'Right to Information'. Right to obtain information is a part of Fundamental Rights under Article 19(1) of the Constitution of India which says that every citizen has freedom of speech and expression. India is a democracy. Every citizen of India pays taxes. Even a beggar on the street pays tax in the form of sales tax, excise duty etc. when he buys a piece of soap or salt from the market. The citizens therefore, have a right to know how their money is being spent and how efficiently and honestly the government employees are working.

Let us first understand the rights available under RTI Act and who is covered under RTI. The RTI Act, 2005 extends to the whole of India except Jammu and Kashmir. All bodies/organisations which are constituted under the Constitution or under any law or under any Government notification, including non-government and private organisations, which are owned, controlled or substantially financed by the Government are covered under the Act. Right to Information Act empowers every citizen to:

- Ask any questions from the government or seek any information;

- Take notes, extracts or certified copies of documents or records;

- Inspect any government works, documents, records;

- Take certified samples of materials of any government work for testing;

- Obtain information in the form of diskettes, floppies, tapes, video cassettes or any other electronic mode or through printouts where such information is stored in any computer or any other device.

However, as per Section 8 of the RTI Act, certain types of information are exempt from being provided under an RTI application. Some of the exemptions have been listed below:

Any information which would affect the sovereignty, integrity, and strategic interests of the Indian State are exempt.

Disclosure of any information which would constitute contempt of court, or which has been expressly barred from publication by any tribunal, or the disclosure of which would cause a breach of privilege of Parliament or State Legislature.

Information which is made available to a person in capacity of their fiduciary relationship with someone.

Information which is personal information the disclosure of which would not have any public interest would be exempt as it would cause an unwarranted breach of privacy.

Government of India has enacted "Right to Information Act 2005" to provide for setting out the practical regime of right to information for citizens to secure access to information under the control of the Public Authorities in order to promote transparency and accountability in the working of any public authority. Section 4 of the RTI Act mandates every public authority or government organisation to maintain all its records duly catalogued and indexed in a manner and the form which facilitates the right to get information and ensure that are appropriate to be computerized and connected through network all over the country on different systems so that access to such records is facilitated. It also states that all information shall be disseminated widely and in such form and manner which is easily accessible to the public. How this Act can be taken advantage of for the benefit of people at large would become clear from the following examples of real life situation.

State Bank of Bikaner & Jaipur

I came to know about this piece of legislation after my retirement from State Bank of Bikaner & Jaipur in 2007. At the time of retirement I was having some pending issue regarding short reimbursement of LTC bill which I submitted to the bank in 2006 while I was in service. The dealing officer was expecting something from me for the difference payment. After studying Right to Information Act, I wrote an application to the bank and sought following information from Delhi Regional Office of the bank in Delhi:

1. Who is the officer in charge looking into LTC matters and for that matter reimbursement of bills?

2. What is the basis of calculation of making reimbursement @ Rs.19290.00 per person? Please provide me certified copy of rules and calculation sheet.

3. What is the progress of my representation as stated above and when I will be paid the difference amount?'

After about 15 days of my sending application, I received a phone call from my friend at the Regional Office. He told me that my file was being searched. I told him the story and requested him to let me know the progress in the matter. He asked me what I would do if my application was not replied to. I informed him about the appeal procedure under the law and warned to send appeal to Head Office at Jaipur in case no reply received within 30 days period as stipulated in the RTI Act. The very next day he told me that my account has been credited with the difference amount Rs. 4530.00 and the information sought would reach me within set time. Finally I got the reply along with the difference amount, though the reply was vague. Why would they accept the mistake?

RTI-REPLY

STATE BANK OF BIKANER AND JAIPUR
REGION-II, DELHI ZONE

Letter No. AGM/II/MISC.

DATED: 03.12.2007

REGISTERED A. D

Shri S. P. Manchanda

Flat No. C2/35B, Keshav Puram, Delhi-110035

Sir,

Sub: Information under Right to Information Act, 2005

This has reference to your letter dated 16/10/2007 requesting for some information under the RTI Act, 2005. Your request has been considered in the light of the provisions of this Act, and accordingly we advise as under:-

1. The officer in charge looking after LFC matters and reimbursement of bills is a Chief Manager in Grade Scale-SMGS-IV.

2. We have since conveyed our approval to Khari Baoli, Delhi Branch to reimburse you a further sum of Rs. 4530/- on account of difference amount of the LFC bill.

3. The reimbursement had been calculated and made based on Notional Air Fare by Indian Airlines from Delhi to

    Embrace Your Own Power to Fight Corruption

Trivandrum and back.

We hope the above satisfies your queries.

However, if you so desire, you can prefer an appeal against this order to the Appellate Authority within 30 days of the receipt of this letter, whose details are given below:

1. Name of the Appellate Authority: General Manager (P & D)
2. Address of the Appellate Authority: State Bank of Bikaner and Jaipur

Head Office, Tilak Marg
Jaipur, Rajasthan
Yours truly,

Central Public Information Officer

State Bank of Bikaner & Jaipur

Zonal Office, Ahimsa Bhawan, New Delhi-110060

Reserve Bank of India

During my service in State Bank I was wondering increase in unclaimed deposits in different banks in India and negative attitude of banks in paying back the money to the legitimate owners or their legal heirs. Can you think of magnitude of unclaimed deposits in various banks in India? In 2007 I requested Reserve Bank of India Mumbai to provide me detailed information about unclaimed monies held by different banks and the RBI guidelines to banks about repayment and the procedure how to utilize the huge funds by banks. Within 30 days of my application under

RTI Act, I received a letter from RBI with the information that about Rs. 1350 crore was lying unclaimed in different banks. RBI provided me information in detail about the amounts of unclaimed deposits each bank was holding. I was also informed that there was no specific policy advised to banks how they should utilize the funds and that the banks were using these deposits in normal business activity (borrowing and lending). After getting information as above, I sent a complaint to Finance Ministry, RBI and Indian Banks Association to formulate policy to reduce huge amount of unclaimed deposits by payment to true owners or legal heirs, and if they are not traceable, transfer the unclaimed monies to Consumer Welfare Fund or Investor Education and Protection Fund. I also filed a complaint before the National Commission for an appropriate order. Within a few days, the Reserve Bank of India issued a notification/circular on 22.08.2008 to all public and private sector banks including foreign banks operating in India with guidelines to find the depositors or their legal heirs proactively and pay them their amount as per the bank's rules. RBI also advised me that Banking Regulation Act is required to be amended for transferring the funds to Consumer Protection Fund. The Indian Banks Association (IBA) informed that they are examining the feasibility of creating a database to enable the customers find their deposits and claim accordingly.

Municipal Corporation of Delhi

When there was undue delay in the construction of underpass near Britannia Chowk, I filed an RTI application with MCD to know the reasons and the people involved in the project. Municipal Corporation of Delhi vide its letter No. EE (PR-III)/RZ/2009-10/1625 dated 14/12/2009 provided me following information:

"… The construction work of underpass near Britannia Chowk was approved by MCD in 2000 and initial project estimate amounted to Rs. 20.58 crores. Revised estimate Rs. 33.97 crores was approved in August 2006. The details of the expenditure made till October 2009 is as under:

Incurred by MCD	Rs. 12.02 crores
Paid to Railways	Rs. 11.54 crores
Paid to DJB	Rs. 1.76 crores
Paid to NDPL	Rs. 2.12 crores

Mr. J.B. Bhatia (E.E.) 9717788319, Mr. Sandeep Sharma (A.E.) 9717788548, Mr. Manoj Gupta (J.E.) 9717788358 and Mr. Rajesh Parashar (J.E.) 9717788738 are presently supervising the said work. The project was delayed due to completion of work by the Railways and non-shifting of services by NDPL, DJB & MTNL etc. and the RUB approaches work is likely to be completed in January 2010 and will be opened to the traffic."

Municipal Corporation Delhi

We are facing problem of stray animals in all areas across Delhi. On 23.04.2009 I sent an RTI application to the Assistant Commissioner/PIO, MCD, Rohini Zone asking various questionsviz. names and contact details of officers responsible for removing stray animals, number of stray dogs caught last year, annual budget of Municipal dog squad, complaints received from various persons in this regard etc. etc. The PIO vide his reply dated 15/05/2009 provided almost all information. The PIO also provided name of officer, Shri Narendra Dabas with phone number 27056512 which I forwarded to Resident Welfare Association for putting up on the notice board. MCD also came into action after that as its officers were not active so far.

State Bank of India

Mr. Rathi was having fixed deposits to the tune of Rs.4 lacs in State Bank of India, Keshav Puram Delhi when he suddenly passed away in 2008. When his wife went to the Bank for collecting his funds, she was told to bring legal representation as there was no nomination in the fixed deposit account. Mrs Rathi came to me and showed me the fixed deposit receipts. I noted that there was indeed nomination number marked on the receipts. When this fact was brought to the notice of the bank manager, he told that there were no nomination papers available pertaining to this number and so the payment would be made to legal heir only if she proves legal representation from the court. The payment was refused for about a year. When the requests and representations did not work, I decided to use RTI Act as a tool. An RTI-application was sent to the Branch Manager asking information about the nomination provided in this account and the name of nominee as per records citing the number of nomination. We also asked the name and designation of employee for safe keeping of nomination papers and action taken by the bank against the employee for misplacing the said documents. Further we asked the names and designation of the officers for not taking action on her requests and representations till date. The bank immediately came into action and searched the nomination documents. Mrs. Rathi was called for completing formalities and payment with interest was made within a week of writing RTI application.

Sant Longowal Institute of Engineering & Technology

Sant Longowal Institute of Engineering & Technology had issued advertisement for some vacant posts of professors through notification No. 01/2012 DATED 23/02/2012. But the candidates were not called for interview until 30thOctober 2012, when I filed RTI application asking questions, e.g. number of candidates applied/rejected for each post, total fee collected for each post, name of the bank and account number in which above funds held and interest earned, dates of interview held and candidates selected/appointed for each post till date, reasons for delay in holding interview with file noting etc. The PIO tried to avoid providing information but furnished some information after first appeal, stating that no interviews held till December 2012. However, on 22/01/2013 the registrar advertised in newspapers for fresh applications from previous applicants without further fees and the interview process started May 2013.

Income Tax Office

Mrs Anju Chadha filed income tax return for assessment year 2008-09 (PAN AJPPC2559N) on 10/11/2009 and the same was acknowledged under ref. 2520131861, claiming refund Rs. 3686.00. When she failed to get refund after more than one and half years, she approached me for grievance solving. On 16/05/2011, I filed RTI application with the I.Tax Department asking names, designation and contact details of officers who were supposed to take action but who have not done so, or have not adhered to the time limits and the present status of the matter. I further enquired complete procedure followed when such an application for refund is received by the department and citizens' charter or rules for taking time for refund applications. I was astonished when Mrs Anju Chadha informed me about receipt of refund within 15 days of filing RTI-application.

Passport Office

My relatives, Akanksha Bakshiand applied for 'tatkal' passports on 30/11/2010 but failed to get their passports even after two months. I checked status and filed RTI application on 28/01/2011 with Regional Passport Office, Hudco Trikoot, Bhikaji Cama Place, New Delhi – 110066 and sought following information:

Please let me know the progress made on their applications till the date of your reply;

Please inform me name of the police station/department to which application was referred for police verification with outward number, date of dispatch and date when reply was received by you;

Please let me know if the department requires any other document/fees for issue of passports;

Please let me know when they are likely to receive the passports. If passports have already been sent please inform me the number and date of dispatch, etc.

I was pleased when Mr Bakshi telephoned me receipt of their passport after about a fortnight.

Delhi Pollution Control Committee

Shri J.P. Sharma, R/o H.No.4621-B/14, Jai Mata Market, Tri Nagar, Delhi was facing problem of pollution created by the owner of House No. 4621-A/14, Jai Mata Market, Tri Nagar Delhi and complained the pollution department for necessary action. When there was no action for 6 months, I suggested him to write application under RTI act. On 11/04/2011 he filed the RTI-application with The Environment Engineer/PIO,Delhi Pollution Control Committee,4th Floor, ISBT Building,Kashmiri Gate, Delhi-110006and sought information about status of his

    Embrace Your Own Power to Fight Corruption

complaint filed and names & contact details of officials looking into his complaint etc. Within one month of filing this RTI application he got reply that action had been taken against the erring person and he had been warned to shift his industry somewhere else. This was also done soon.

Horticultural Department

An application No. 23(16)/HD M-324/PWD/508 dated 8/11/2010 was sent by the Deputy Director (Hort.) Hort. Division M-324 PWD (GOD) New Delhi to the Deputy Conservator of Forest, West forest Division, Mandir Lane, New Delhi – 110060 requesting permission for trimming of Eucalyptus trees from Metro pillar No.239 to 258 Keshav Puram side. Since the needful not done for months, I sought the following information on 12/02/2011 under RTI Act:

Whether the Hort. Department has received any communication from PWD granting permission of above-mentioned trees in response to letter dated 8.11.2010 and previous letter dated 3.3.2010?

If the permission has been accorded, please let me know when the trimming work would begin? Please also send me photocopy of the letter of permission received.

If no communication received, please inform me if any reminder forwarded to PWD for doing the needful.

Please let me know if the permission has been denied by the PWD and also furnish me photocopy of the same.

I got the requisite information after about a month, stating that trimming work had already started.

Delhi Subordinate Staff Selection Board (DSSSB)

Finding that Delhi Subordinate Staff Selection Board New Delhi has not invited candidates for test after one year of accepting application and collecting huge fees, I sent RTI application to know the reason of delay in taking examination. When proper information was not provided I filed first appeal and then second appeal before Central Information Commission. The CIC ordered on 24.06.2011 as under:

CENTRAL INFORMATION COMMISSION

Club Building (Near Post Office)
Old JNU Campus, New Delhi - 110067
Tel: +91-11-26161796

Decision No. CIC/SG/A/2011/001104/13058
Appeal No. CIC/SG/A/2011/001104

Relevant facts emerging from the Appeal:

Appellant :   Mr. S.P. Manchanda,

C-2/35 B, Keshav Puram,

Delhi - 110035

Respondent: Mr. V. K. Bansal

PIO & Dy. Secretary,

Delhi Subordinate Selection Services Board,

DSSSB, Government of N.C.T. of Delhi,

Karkadooma, New Delhi 110092

RTI application filed on   :   17/02/2011

PIO replied on   :   01/03/2011

First Appeal filed on   :   03/03/2011

First Appellate Authority order of :   01/04/2011

Second Appeal received on   :   20/04/2011

Sl.	Information Sought Reply of PIO	Information Sought Reply of PIO
1.	With respect to the advertisement No. 01/2010, some vacancies for the post of teacher were advertised and examinations were to be held on specific dates. How many total candidates applied and the total fee amount collected in the shape of Indian Postal order from the appellants with their application?	As per advertisement No. 1/2010, total 255848 candidates have applied for the post of teachers under post code of 01/2010 to 18/2010. Total examination fee Rs 17605900 collected in the form at IPO's DDS.
2.	The year for which these vacancies were notified as per above advertisement.	The candidate is required to submit the requisite fee of Rs 30/- (@ Rs-2/- per copy) for the details of post published in advertisement No. 01/2010 which contains the requisite information. Informations ought is not available in compiled form.
3.	Specific reasons for not holding examinations.	DSSB conducts examination after putting in place all basic requirements and administrative facilities required for conduct of examination. As soon as these requirements are fulfilled, the schedule for this examination shall be announced.

4.	Any future date(s) of said examination.	The new schedule for the posts of teachers has not been decided so far. As soon as the date for the said examination is notified, the same will be published in the leading newspapers and also uploaded on the official website of DSSSB i.e.www.dsssb.delhigovt.nic.in
5.	By when the date(s) of future examination will be decided by DSSSB.	The new schedule for the posts of teachers has not been decided so far. As soon as the date for the said examination is notified, the same will be published in the leading newspapers and also uploaded on the official website of DSSSB i.e.www.dsssb.delhigovt.nic.in
5.		As same as point No. 3.
6.	The competent authority who will decide the date(s) of future examination.	The schedule of the examination is decided by the Board with approval of Chairman of the Board.
7.	The policy whether candidates are informed individually by post about the future examination once the examination is postponed due to any reason.	The schedule of the examination will be published in the leading newspapers and also uploaded on the official website as mentioned in point No. 4.

Embrace Your Own Power to Fight Corruption

8.	If there is no examination in the near future,policy whether the fees will be refunded to the candidates.	Not pertains to this branch.
9.	Last date of the updating of the website of DSSB in the year 2010 and 2011.	Not pertains to examination.

Grounds for the First Appeal

The information provided was incomplete.

Order of the First Appellate Authority (FAA)

FAA observed that the information sought was provided but it was incomplete. Since the information asked for pertained to various branches of DSSSB, they would recheck and re-ensure the information as per records and would send the same to the appellant within 10 working days.

Ground of the Second Appeal

Information provided was not satisfactory.

Relevant Facts emerging during Hearing

The following were present

Appellant: Mr. S.P. Manchanda on telephone through mobile no. 9891827669;

Respondent: Mr. V. K. Bansal, PIO & Dy. Secretary;

The respondent has not given appropriate information regarding query, 2, 3, 8 & 9 as discussed with the Appellant and the respondent. The Commission directs the respondent to give appropriate answers to query 2, 3, 8 & 9. The appellant also states that the website of the department does not function properly. DSSSB should look into this and ensure that the website is operating properly.

Decision: The Appeal is allowed.

The PIO is directed to provide the information as directed above to the Appellant before 10 July 2011.

This decision is announced in open chamber.

Notice of this decision be given free of cost to the parties.

Any information in compliance with this Order will be provided free of cost as per Section 7(6) of RTI Act.

Shailesh Gandhi

Information Commissioner

24 June 2011

Delhi Development Authority

An RTI application was filed on 13th February 2010 with Delhi Development Authority (DDA) to know the status of application requesting conversion of flat from leasehold to freehold located in C-1 Block, Keshav Puram Delhi. The DDA officer asked for some Challans of installments deposited in 1973 for doing the needful. I filed an appeal to know the details of pending installments, if any and the exact amount with interest & penalty to be deposited as per DDA records. DDA informed the amount to be deposited subject to verification of two Challans. I was also told to visit DDA office for further information and doing the needful. I informed the

DDA that I was seeking information from DDA under RTI Act stating that RTI law gives the right to the citizen of India to seek information from public authority and definitely not the other way round' Further I asked about the time periods when the accounts of DDA were audited in their office and whether DDA sought explanation from the delinquent employees for non-reconciliation of accounts since 1973. Finally, the Deputy Director, DDA agreed to my request and issued letter on 23rd September, 2010 that 'report submitted by the Accounts Branch....you are requested to deposit a sum of Rs.828/- upto 31.10.2010 so that freehold.... could be processed.'

Prime Minister Office

When I came to know about fraud committed by some employees in PMO, I sent an RTI application to know the details of fraud and steps taken by PMO to check such types of frauds in future. PMO vide letter No. RTI/463/2009-PMA dated 19.03.2009 provided following information in addition to staff details:

"…No periodicity of audit of accounts has been specified. The internal audit of accounts were carried out in February 2008 before the fraud in question by Ministry of Personnel, Public Grievances and Pensions. The following were members of the audit party:

Shri P.N. Ratra, Sr. AO

Shri Abhay Singh, Sr. AO

Shri Hari Ram, AAO

Shri Naveen Kumar, AAO

The work of the sections has been streamlined. A separate entity in the form of Cash Section has been created. Rotation of officials has been done. Pay bill preparation arrangement has been revamped by way of putting new security checks in the software by

NIC. Other measures in the matters are also underway."

Sub-registrar Office

There was huge black money payment in some property in Tilak Nagar area. On 18/06/2010, I filed RTI application to seek information about sale/purchase value of the property and stamp duty paid on the date of purchase. When complete information was not provided by PIO and FAA, I approached the CIC which allowed my appeal vide decision No. CIC/SG/A/2010/002874/10336 dated 07.12.2010 with following directions:

"The appeal is allowed. The PIO is directed to facilitate an inspection of the relevant records by the Applicant on 29th and 30th December, 2010 from 10.00 AM onwards. The PIO will give attested photocopies of records which the Appellant wants free of cost upto 10 pages.

The Commission also directs Divisional Commissioner to send his views on about putting property transactions on the website as directed above to the Commission before 25 December 2010."

The next day many newspapers published this news affirming that CIC is contemplating to make public all property transactions taking place in the national capital and has sought the views of the Delhi Government on it.

Chaudhary Charan Singh University

Chaudhary Charan Singh University (CCS University) had poorly maintained website and the students were not getting proper information about dates of examination and results declared. Their queries were not answered satisfactorily on telephone. The letters were never replied. Personal visits to Meerut were also futile many a times. On 4th Sept. 2009, I sought information from the CCS University and asked following questions under RTI Act;

"...what steps have been taken by your university to meet its obligation under section 4(1) (a)....please let me know the date/s of instructions/orders received from superior authorities mentioning name/s, with respect to implementation...... and updating the website of CCS University with reference to RTI Act."

After about 4 months of my application and the appeal, I was informed by PIO, CCS University vide letter dated 8.3.2010 that CCS University has updated its website after uploading requisite information on 16 points as provided in the RTI Act and all desired information is now available on the website for use of general public/students. The students are not only getting information about the examination results and dates of admission, they are now filling their admission forms online and are not required to visit Meerut again and again for fulfilling formalities regarding admissions. RTI application was sent in larger public interest and it served the purpose to great extent.

चौधरी चरण सिंह विश्वविद्यालय, मेरठ
Ch. Charan Singh University, Meerut

पत्रांक : जनसूचना/862/4371

दिनाँक : 8-3-2010

श्री एस0पी0 मन्चन्दा,

सी 2/35 बी, केशव पुरम,

दिल्ली–110035।

महोदय,

कृपया आपके पत्र दिनांक 04.09.2009 जिसमें सूचना के अधिकार अधिनियम, 2005 के अंतर्गत अधिनियम के सैक्शन 4(1)ए के सम्बन्ध में सूचना मांगी है, का सन्दर्भ ग्रहण करें। बिन्दुवार सूचना निम्नवत है:

बिंदु 1: विश्वविद्यालय द्वारा सूचना के अधिकार अधिनियम, 2005 के सैक्शन 4(1)ए के सम्बन्ध में कुल 16 बिन्दुओं की सूचना तैयार कर विश्वविद्यालय की वेबसाईट ूूबेनदपअमतेपजलण्बण्पद पर अपलोड करा दी गयी है। जो कि जनसामान्य के लिये उपलब्ध है। आप विश्वविद्यालय वेबसाईट से प्राप्त कर सकते हैं। विश्वविद्यालय विभिन्न विभागों द्वारा सूचनाओं को व्यवस्थित रूप से संकलित किया जाता है जैसे परीक्षा विभाग द्वारा परीक्षा सम्बन्धी, मान्यता विभाग द्वारा महाविद्यालयों/संस्थानों की मान्यता, गोपनीय विभाग द्वारा परीक्षा परिणाम सम्बन्धी सूचनाओं एवं रिकॉर्ड को व्यवस्थित रूप से संकलित किया जाता है।

    Embrace Your Own Power to Fight Corruption

भवदीय,

प्रभारी, जनसूचना विभाग

Department of Urban Development

Every MLA in Delhi gets two crores of rupees every year to spend on works for the development of constituency. This is the people's money. MLAs should ask from the people of their constituencies before taking decisions on how this money should be spent. However, most of the time, this consultation is not done and money is spent on works which benefit MLAs and which may not a high priority for the people. I filed RTI application in September 2009 with the Govt. of NCT of Delhi, Department of Urban Development (Planning Branch) Delhi Sectt. to seek detailed information about the amount spent last year in our constituency. I got the following reply from the public information officer:

"Rs. 85 lakhs were available with MLA in his kitty at the beginning of current financial year in Wazirpur Assembly Constituency. He was provided Rs. 200 lacs more during this current year. The following funds were released to Executing Agencies (out of Rs. 285 lacs) during 2009-10 upto 27/11/2009:

DDA	Rs. 31.54 lacs
MCD	Rs. 181.63 lacs
DJB	Rs. 33.60 lacs
NDPL	Rs. 28.33 lacs
Slum& JJ	Rs. 09.90 lacs

After getting the requisite information, I contacted RWA president for pending works which can be allocated from funds still available with MLA. Every citizen has right to getthe information on funds available with MLA but also audit expenses under Right to Information Act.

Postal Department

If any person wants to send RTI-application to some department/ ministry of the Central Government, he can also submit his application together with RTI fee (without postal charges) at any authorised post office and get acknowledgement of submitting the same. The post office acts as assistant public information officer and takes responsibility to forward the application to the concerned public authority without payment of postal fee viz. speed post or regd. post fee. One day when I reached the post office at about 2 pm, the clerk refused to accept the application stating that applications can be accepted before 2 pm only. Next days I took four RTI applications with an application in the name of post office asking the time of accepting application for speed post, registered post, lunch time etc. and whether time displayed accordingly at some prominent place. I also sought information about late attendance by the staff. All the four applications were accepted by the counter clerk happily as I reached at 11.00 am that day. When I visited the post office after a fortnight, I noticed some change in the post office. Notice boards displayed at prominent place about different

 Embrace Your Own Power to Fight Corruption

timings, one board stating that 'RTI applications are accepted here'. Of course, the staff was punctual and courteous too. After few days I got following information to my RTI application dated 30.12.2008:

"1. Yes, necessary instructions on the subject have been issued to all post offices....

The timing of acceptance of RTI applications has been displayed in all the post offices.....

Time for receiving registered post, speed post and RTI applications is as under.....

Name & designation of all the staff working in Onkar Nagar post office along with their date of joining is furnished in the enclosed Annexure. Photocopy of attendance for the month of December 2008 is enclosed...."

Corporation Bank

One of my friends wanted to know the account details of his grandfather in the Corporation Bank Chandni Chowk Branch. His grandfather died about 20 years ago and my friend believed his grandfather might have left some money in his saving bank and fixed deposit accounts. The Manager refused to oblige as my friend was not having pass book, not even the account number. He contacted me and I filed RTI-application for furnishing information on unclaimed deposits in the bank with the names and addresses of depositors. The PIO of the bank denied information stating that the information is held by the bank in fiduciary capacity. First appeal also was not successful. Then I filed 2nd appeal before the Central Information Commission and the Information Commissioner ordered the Corporation Bank to furnish number of accounts and amount of unclaimed deposits held with Chandni Chowk Branch Delhi and to provide copy of RBI/GoI guidelines governing the procedure to be adopted by the banks in dealing with unclaimed accounts. "The issue raised by the Applicant is in regard to the unclaimed accounts lying for 10 years or more in various branches of banks need to be looked at by the RBI and other authorities very seriously and an appropriate scheme devised to deal with such sums of money.", commented Chief Information Commissioner, Shri Satyananda Mishra in his order dated 11th November, 2009.

Punjab National Bank

Some of my relative was holding saving bank account in Punjab National Bank in Janakpuri branch about 13 years ago when he went missing from Haridwar. Police complaint was filed by the family but could not be traced till now. As the account holder was not 'dead' as per any record, the bank refused to pay the amount to the family presuming he might return and claim his funds. When his son contacted me in 2010, I advised him to write an RTI-application asking the balance amount in the account, nomination detailsand the procedure for claiming amount in such cases. The bank informed that about Rs. 25000/- was lying in his account at the time when missing report was submitted in the bank and no nomination details were filed. For claiming this amount he was advised to move competent court and bring orders for payment, as there was no procedure for payment to legal heirs in such cases. However, the law says that a person is presumed as 'dead' when he is not traceable after 7 years of filing missing report with the police. So we filed claim documents with the bank on this base and requested refund of amount with interest. The bank insisted legal representation from competent court. We filed RTI applications in the Reserve Bank of India as well as Punjab National Bank asking the procedure for payment of small amounts and threshold limit prescribed by Reserve Bank of India for payment without legal process. Within a month requisite information was received stating that payment in such cases allowed upto Rs. 1 lakh against indemnity letter only. Finally the bank paid the amount Rs.61000/- with interest after execution of indemnity bond.

Medical Council of India

We are aware of medical negligence and corruption in the hospitals & nursing homes. I filed a complaint of medical negligence by the Max Hospital Pitampura and subsequently issued an RTI application to the Medical Council of India to know the status of complaint. When the information was not forthcoming in mandatory 30/35 days, first appeal was filed before the Secretary, Medical Council of India. There was no response from first appellate authority too. Then I approached Central Information Commission with a second appeal. CIC decided the matter on 9th may 2012 as under:

"….The PIO is directed to provide the information on query 05 to the Appellant before 30 May 2012. The PIO is also directed to ensure that a cheque of Rs.3000/- as compensation is sent to the Appellant before 30 June 2012.

The PIO is directed to ensure that the information as directed above are displayed on the website of the Council before 30 May 2012 and is updated regularly every month.

These directions are being given by the Commission under its powers under Section 19(8) (a)(iii) of the RTI Act. It is also in conformance with the requirements of Section 4(1)(b) (xvii)…."

CENTRAL INFORMATION COMMISSION

Club Building (Near Post Office)
Old JNU Campus, New Delhi - 110067
Tel: +91-11-26161796

Decision No. CIC/SG/A/2012/000876/18840
Appeal No. CIC/SG/A/2012/000876

Relevant Facts emerging from the Appeal

Appellant	:	Mr. S. P. Mancharida
		C-2/ 35 B, Keshav Puram
		Delhi-110035
Respondent	:	Mr. Davinder Kumar
		Public Information Officer
		& Joint Secretary
		Medical Council of India,
		O/o The Medical council of India,
		Pocket-14, Sec-8, Dwarka,
		New Delhi – 110077

RTI application filed on : 12/01/2012 recd on 18/01/2012

PIO replied	:	05/03/2012
First Appeal	:	24/02/2012
First Appellate Authority order:		Not mentioned
Second Appeal received on :		14/03/2012

Ethics Committee had held four doctors of Max Hospital, Pitampura guilty of medical negligence/misconduct at its meeting of 8/3/2011. It was stated that quantum of punishment will be decided at the next ethics committee meeting.

Sl.	Information Sought
1.	What punishment was ordered against each of the four doctors?
2.	When did punishment ordered?
3.	If punishment has not been yet ordered, the reason thereof.
4.	Please let me know the present status in this case,
5.	Please inform me all correspondence/emails MCI had between Max Hospital & its doctors, Ethics Committee & its members, Board of Governors of MCI and any other organization/individual in this regard after 08-03.2011. Please also provide file noting.
PIO's Reply:	
Matter is under consideration	

Grounds for the First Appeal

Information provided has not been provided.

Order of the FAA

Not mentioned.

Grounds for the Second Appeal

Information provided is incomplete and unsatisfactory

Relevant Facts emerging during Hearing

The following were present

Appellant: Mr. S. P. Mancharida

Respondent: Mr. Anuj Kumar, Section Officer and Mr. Saurabh

Chawla, Advocate on behalf of Mr. Davinder Kumar, Public Information Officer & Joint Secretary;

The Appellant has sought information about 04 doctors who have been found guilty of Medical Negligence/Misconduct by the Ethics Committee of MCI in a meeting held on 08/03/2011. The Appellant has been informed about this in RTI by MCI. In the present case he had sought information about the punishment in this matter. According to the Ethics Committee meeting held on 08/03/2011 the quantum of punishment was to be decided in the next meeting. The respondents state that the Ethics Committee meets every month. Thus over 12 or 13 meetings have been held and the matter of punishment is claimed to have been still under consideration. Since the Ethics Committee is delaying giving the punishment contrary to its own decision, information regarding the first four queries cannot be given. However, the PIO has given no explanation for denying information on query-5. Refusal of any information in RTI has to be based under Section 8(1) of the RTI Act. The PIO is directed to provide information on query-5 asper available records to the Appellant since no ground for denial has been established. The Appellant points out that this is a case of medical negligence which resulted in his daughter's death in May 2009. He is naturally aggrieved and has been pursuing the matter in the MCI since last two years. The Ethics Committee of MCI has reportedly found 04 doctors guilty but is now delaying awarding any punishment since past 14 months. The complete collapse of mechanisms to punish people who have been found guilty is extremely damaging for society and denies victims a sense of justice being done. The Commission realizes that the Appellant has been harassed by not being provided information on query-5 without any reasons. He has had to pursue this appeal and come to the Commission unnecessarily.

     Embrace Your Own Power to Fight Corruption

Harassment of a common man by public authorities is socially abhorring and legally impermissible. It may harm him personally but the injury to society is far more grievous. Crime and corruption thrive and prosper in the society due to lack of public resistance. Nothing is more damaging than the feeling of helplessness. An ordinary citizen instead of complaining and fighting succumbs to the pressure of undesirable functioning in offices instead of standing against it. Therefore the award of compensation for harassment by public authorities not only compensates the individual, satisfies him personally but helps incuring social evil. It may result in improving the work culture and help in changing the outlook.

The Commission therefore awards a compensation to the Complainant of Rs.3000/- as per the provisions of Section 19(8) (b) of the RTI Act for the loss and detriment suffered by him in pursing the appeal and getting the information late.

The Right to Information is a fundamental right of the citizens which has been codified by the RTI act,No. 22 of 2005. The act envisions that all citizens shall receive information primarily by suo moto disclosures by various public authorities as prescribed by section (4) of the act. Disclosures in accordance with the said Section are crucial to ensure transparency and accountability in institutions. This would reduce the load of RTI Applications being filed with each institution as information would be freely available to citizens and they would not have to apply for it. It further envisages that citizens would be required to specifically ask for information under section (6) only in a few cases. Citizens have been demanding that certain information is essential to them and should be available pro-actively in form of public notice boards, display boards etc.

It is necessary that information about names of doctors who are found guilty by the Ethics Committee of Medical Negligence/

Misconduct are displayed on the website of the Medical Council of India and when the punishment, is decided the quantum of punishment should also be displayed. The PIO will ensure that the names of doctors who have been found guilty by the Ethics Committee since January 2011 are displayed on the website of the MCI and the quantum of punishment is also displayed whenever it is decided.

This shall be displayed in the following format

Sl.	Date of Ethics Committee meeting when medical negligence/ misconduct has been established.	Name of Doctor & Address	Quantum of Punishment	Date of Ethics Meeting in which Quantum of punishment was decided.

This list will be updated every month.

Decision:

The Appeal is allowed.

The PIO is directed to provide the information on query 05 to the Appellant before30 May 2012. The PIO is also directed to ensure that a cheque of Rs.3000/- as compensation is sent to the Appellant before 30 June 2012.

The PIO is directed to ensure that the information as directed above are displayed on the website of the Council before 30 May 2012 and is updated regularly every month.

These directions are being given by the Commission under its powers under Section 19(8)(a)(iii) of the RTI Act. It is also in conformance with the requirements of Section 4(1)(b)(xvii).

The PIO will send a consolidated report of compliance of the above directions to the Commission by 05 June 2012. The report may be sent to rtimonitoring@gmail.com, with a copy to the Complainant.

This decision is announced in open chamber.

Notice of this decision be given free of cost to the parties.

Any information in compliance with this Order will be provided free of cost as per Section 7(6) of RTI Act.

Shailesh Gandhi

Information Commissioner

09 May 2012

(In any correspondence on this decision, mention the complete decision number.) (PG)

Revenue Department

It is common knowledge that a person cannot purchase immovable property in Delhi without involvement of black money. Due to undervaluation, there is huge evasion of stamp duty and loss to exchequer. In March 2011, I filed RTI-application with the PIO, Revenue Department, Sham Nath Marg, Delhi asking criteria, calculation and methodology for fixing circle rates in Delhi. I also sought information about rules framed under Stamp Act. When I was informed that there were no criteria, calculation or methodology for revision of circle rates, I sent complaint letter to the Divisional Commissioner, Chief Minister, Lt. Governor etc. for taking steps to rationalise the rates. In November, 2011 and then in December 2012, the Government increased circle rates but circle rates were increased illogically and arbitrarily. Circle rates in posh areas like Vasant Kunj are much less than the prevailing market rates and there is rampant undervaluation, on the other hand circle rates in backward areas like Narela are more than double the circle rates and people are forced to pay double the legitimate stamp duty. My RTI-application was considered as one of the best applications by the Information Commissioner in his order dated 11.1.2015. When nothing happened, I again filed RTI application dated 11.02.2017 and the matter was escalated to Central Information Commission. On 11.08.2017 CIC heard me and the respondent PIO. CIC allowed my appeal and directed the PIO to provide complete information as also inspection of record. Based on the revealing information received from the revenue department, I filed PIL before the Delhi High Delhi in May 2019. Notice was issued to GNCTD to file Affidavit and the government counsel accepted the anomaly and assured the Hon'ble Chief Justice to rationalise circle rates as early as possible on scientific basis. Let us hope the government rationalises circle rates soon in larger public interest.

CENTRAL INFORMATION COMMISSION
August Kranti Bhawan, Bhikaji Cama Place,
New Delhi-110066

F. No. CIC/OOCMD/A/2017/144279

Date of Hearing	:	11.08.2017
Date of Decision	:	11.08.2017
Appellant/Complainant	:	Mr. S P Manchanda
Respondent	:	PIO

Sub-Divisional, Revenue Department, GNCTD

Through:- Sh. P R Kaushik-SDM-I

Information Commissioner: Shri Yashovardhan Azad

Relevant facts emerging from appeal:

RTI application filed on   :   11.02.2017

PIO replied on   :   15.02.2017

First Appeal filed on   :   13.04.2017

First Appellate Order on   :   12.05.2017

2nd Appeal/complaint received on: 29.06.2017

Information sought and background of the case:

Vide RTI application dated 11.02.2017, the appellant sought following information:

1. Details of action taken on each aspect of enclosed submissions routed through Public Grievance Monitoring System of Delhi Govt. and Email, by the concerned authority where submission might have been forwarded and particulars of follow-up action.

2. Was my submissions placed before Hon'ble Chief Minister of Delhi and Dy. Chief Minister for consideration? If so, complete information after placing these submissions before them and action taken by them.

3. Number of complaints and suggestion received by Govt. of NCT of Delhi after advertisement published on 27.07.2016 in some newspapers for submitting suggestions till 16.08.2016 for revision of circle rates. Please let me know their names and addresses.

4. Action taken by the government after receipt of suggestions from public for rationalization of circle rates in Delhi.

5. Circular/notification issued by the government regarding circle rates after receipt of suggestion from public in this regard.

6. After receiving information, I would like to inspect files in this connection. Please let me know the date and time

convenient for inspection of record.

The PIO, Dy. Secretary transferred the RTI application to the PIO, O/o Dy. C.M. (Minister Revenue), PIO, Div. Commissioner, GNCTD and PIO, NDMC, Civic Centre vide letter dated 15.02.2017. Having not received any information from the CPIOs, the appellant filed first appeal. The FAA directed the SPIO/SDM to furnish proper reply point wise to the appellant within 03 weeks. Feeling aggrieved over non compliance of FAO, the appellant approached the Commission.

Relevant facts emerging during hearing

Both parties are present for hearing. Appellant states that discrepancy between circle rates and market valuation is leading to huge loss to public exchequer since legal transfer of such properties is discouraged and no clear information in this regard is made accessible due to deliberate concealment.

Decision

After hearing parties and perusal of record, the Commission is of the opinion that the appellant deserves to get information regarding the status of Government action on numerous suggestions regarding revision of Circle rates. The Commission notes that this is an important issue and one which addresses a public cause. Accordingly, the Respondent is directed to provide response to the queries of the appellant and allow inspection of all relevant records within three weeks of receipt of this order. The Respondent shall submit a compliance report before the Commission, within a week of carrying out the above said directions.

The appeal is disposed of accordingly.

(Yashovardhan Azad)

 Embrace Your Own Power to Fight Corruption

Authenticated true copy. Additional copies of orders shall be supplied against application and payment of the charges prescribed under the Act to the CPIO of this Commission.

HUDA

My friend Shri Om Parkash Arora is resident of Keshav Puram who retired from Parliament House office in 2001. Immediately after retirement he invested all sums in a plot to be allotted by HUDA in 2005. Although HUDA allotted the plot after collecting full payment in 2002, possession was not given till 2007 when he went to HUDA office at Gurgaon only to be told that his plot would be given in few days. When so many written complaints and representation remained unanswered and his personal visits also futile, he approached me in 2010. I filed an application under RTI Act and asked information about the payments made in 2012 and the reason for long delay in giving possession along with file notings. After about a month, he got information that the plot in question was in dispute with some villagers and the case was pending in High Court since 2000. How can they allot plot in 2002 and collect payment despite dispute of land? After getting desired information, Shri Arora filed a consumer case in District Court Gurgaon in March 2012. After about 4 months, District Forum accepted the complaint and directed HUDA Haryana to give possession of some alternative plot within one month. Finally he got possession of his plot towards the end of 2012. He has to get compensation, interest etc. He has also filed RTI application when he will get compensation, interest and legal expenses as directed by District Consumer Court.

District Consumer Forum

A consumer complaint was filed by me in District Consumer Court Shalimar Bagh, Delhi in October 2012. When the court did not admit my application despite five hearings and lost my file (intentionally), I filed RTI-application on 15 points questioning the working of the consumer court and inefficiency of its President. No response received even after a month and I filed my first appeal before State Commission, Vikas Bhawan New Delhi praying for the desired information and action against the President as per RTI Act. The first appellate authority directed the PIO/President to furnish reply within 15 days. The PIO/President then provided only partial information to me and evaded crucial information. I have approached Central Information Commission now and will ensure that he is fined and compensation paid to me, when he appears for hearing in CIC after about 6 months this year.

Delhi Administration

Mrs Ambika Unny retired as teacher from Delhi Administration in 2009. Although she was paid superannuation funds within 6 months after retirement, some arrear was due because of salary difference decided after her retirement. When all efforts to get payment of arrear failed, she approached me for grievance resolving. I filed RTI-application on 27/11/2012 with the The DDE/PIO, Directorate of Education, District North-West, F.U. Block, Pitampura, Delhi-34and asked the education department about action taken by each of the employees after receipt of her representation. I also asked about the interest on the amount due to delayed payment and names & contact details of officials of the vigilance department. Within one month Mrs Unny got the reply that her payment has been processed and finally, she got the amount of arrear within next 10 days.

     Embrace Your Own Power to Fight Corruption

Dehradun Treasury Office

On 15/10/2012 Shri N.K. Goyal of Keshav Puram, Delhi contacted me for arrears of basic pension and filed RTI-application with The Chief Treasury Officer/PIO,Dehradun Treasury, DEHRADUN– 248001 asking information in reference to his request letter No. 719/PF/NK dated 19/07/2012 addressed to the Chief Treasury Officer for payment of arrears of basic pension w.e.f.01/01/2006 along with D.A. rates granted from time to time in respect of GRD No. o32/3473 (New No. o32S49765). When there was no response after one and half months, I filed first appeal before the first appellate authority. Finally he got the arrear next month and reply that the payment had been processed.

MOP/Central Electricity Regulatory Commission

Information was sought under RTI Act regarding allocation of marks in the area of educational background, experience and interaction during engagement of consultants. Detailed mark-sheet for each candidate was provided. Further, background of members in the selection committee was also asked and furnished. First appeal filed for other queries regarding salaries and procedure adopted at each stage of selection. Delhi High Court had already adjudicated that rejection of person in the panel had to be justified.

Delhi Electricity Regulatory Commission (DERC)

Fuming misappropriation in the accounts, number of questions were asked from DERC by way of RTI application in respect of functioning of electricity distribution companies since they are not under purview of RTI Act due to stay by Delhi High Court. DERC replied that distribution companies have been directed to meter self-consumption in their own premises. Evasion of 5% electricity tax on their own consumption needs to be accounted for along with copy to Municipal Commissioners/ Mayors of MCD for follow-up. Differential rates being charged by MCD versus NDMC stand highlighted on account of government subsidy and major funding in NDMC which is under government control.

Delhi High Court

Having come to know that about 3.6 crores of litigations are pending in the courts across India and over 1 lakh cases pending in the High Court of Delhi, I filed an RTI-application on 17.04.2013 seeking following information from Delhi High Court:

1. Number of vacations in 2010, 2011 and 2012 with reasons.
2. Law/Rule prescribing vacation.
3. Name of Competent authority to decide vacation in a year.
4. Complaint/Suggestion/petition received in above 3 years to reduce vacations….
5. Name of authority competent to reduce vacations."

The PIO of the High Court vide letter dated 10.05.2013 informed that this court observed 210 working days during the years 2010,2011 and 2013….and that Hon'ble the Chief Justice of this Court is the competent authority to decide and reduce the number of vacations. Further, no such complaint/suggestion/ petitions were received in the concerned branch. Armed with above information, I filed a public interest ligation (PIL) in Delhi High Court which will come up for hearing after summer vacation.

Drugs Control Department, GNCTD

Drugs Control Department in Delhi spirals out of control. On 22.02.2016 I sought information regarding provisions of drugs and cosmetics act & rules about the sanctioned and vacant posts of inspectors and number of inspections carried out by the department. When no satisfactory response was received, the matter was escalated to Central Information Commission. After hearing parties and perusal of record, the Commission noted that the query raised by the appellant was indeed in public interest and directed the respondent to provide complete information with inspection of records. Inspection report was required to be sent to the Commission within two days thereafter. Soon thereafter the department filled up vacancies of inspectors and inspection of chemists/shops was ensured for the welfare of community.

CENTRAL INFORMATION COMMISSION
August Kranti Bhawan, Bhikaji Cama Place,
New Delhi-110066

F. No. CIC/ADCND/A/2016/303588

Date of Hearing	:	11.08.2017
Date of Decision	:	11.08.2017
Appellant/Complainant	:	Mr. S P Manchanda

Respondent: Drugs Control Department GNCTD,

Through:- Sh. G K Kapur

Information Commissioner: Shri Yashovardhan Azad

Relevant facts emerging from appeal:

RTI application filed on	:	22.02.2016
PIO replied on	:	22.03.2016
First Appeal filed on	:	18.04.2016
First Appellate Order on	:	02.06.2016

2nd Appeal/complaint received on: 17.09.2016

Information sought and background of the case

Vide RTI application dated 22.02.2016 addressed to Drugs

Control Department, the appellant sought information regarding the provisions of drugs and cosmetics act & rules made thereunder that regulates the manufacture & sale of drugs to ensure quality and availability of drugs at reasonable price. In the respect appellant sought information on 08 points about sanctioned and vacant posts of inspector etc and number of inspection carried out by the department.

The CPIO vide letter dated 22.03.2016 furnished the information enclosing Annexures on point nos. 1, 2, 3, 4 & 7. In response to point no. 5, the CPIO stated that as per statutory requirement to carry out inspection for retail sale/whole sale establishment is once a year and for manufacturing is once year and in response to point no. 6 it was stated that as far as possible inspections are carried out as per details in terms of Annexure-III. Further, in response to point no. 8 the Respondent replied that appellant can inspect the relevant files with prior appointment with the PIO on any working day from Monday to Friday. Dissatisfied with response received from CPIO, the appellant filed first appeal. The FAA upheld the reply/information provided by the CPIO. Feeling aggrieved as dissatisfied and incomplete information received, the appellant approached the Commission.

Relevant facts emerging during hearing

Both parties are present for hearing and the appellant points out that the Respondent department's failure is evident from the consequences faced by public at large. The lives of the people are being threatened due to inaccurate and improper, untested drugs available in the market, which should have been scrutinised much more keenly and inspected by the Respondent authorities. The inspections are carried out only once a year and because of shortfall of staff by 6 persons and the huge growth of population,

 Embrace Your Own Power to Fight Corruption

more stringency cannot be exercised by the Respondent.

Decision: After hearing parties and perusal of record, the Commission notes that the query raised by the appellant is indeed in public interest and the information has been sought in order to safeguard public health at large. It has been accepted by the Respondent that due to the shortage of staff mandatory checks of all the sales premises has not been possible nor even of the manufacturing firms. The statistics provided by the respondents clearly establish the case for filling up the vacant posts in the department as also a proactive approach towards inspection of Drug related establishments.

The Commission finds that the necessary information to the queries has been provided. It is up to the Public Authority to ensure that requisite measures are taken to fill the vacancies in the department and ensure that the required inspections and checks are carried out in the interest of public health/safety. It may also be mentioned here that the appellant has pointed out during the hearing that a glaring anomaly already exists in the system. While the Drugs and Cosmetics Act, 1940 stipulates that only a pharmacy graduate can lead the Drugs Control Department, and the Drug Controller himself is supposed to possess Masters Degree in Pharmacy, Chemistry, Pharmacology with knowledge of drugs and manufacturing, currently the Drug Controller is an IAS officer, with no expertise in this field. Again this is a matter for the Delhi government to ponder upon.

In the light of the foregoing submissions, the Commission hereby directs the Respondent to provide inspection of all the relevant records in parlance with the queries raised by the appellant, within a week of receipt of this order. After inspection of the records is carried out by the appellant, minutes of the said inspection shall be submitted by the Respondent before the Commission within two days thereafter.

The appeal is disposed of accordingly.

(Yashovardhan Azad)
Information Commissioner

Authenticated true copy. Additional copies of orders shall be supplied against application and payment of the charges prescribed under the Act to the CPIO of this Commission.

(R.P. Grover)
Designated Officer

Excise, Entertainment & Luxury Tax Department

Excise Department granted license for opening of 5 liquor shops within a period of 3 years in Keshav Puram area. I sought information on 10 points relating to closing/shifting of the liquor shops situated in residential colony near DEIT/schools. Having received a dis satisfactory reply I filed first appeal and then second appeal before CIC. The Information Commissioner in his order appreciated the appellant for raising an issue of larger public interest and directed the department to give an opportunity to inspect the records so as to allay his concerns and also to provide detailed reply to the appellant within 3 weeks. The matter has been referred to the Hon'ble Chief Minister for necessary action in this regard.

केन्द्रीयसूचनाआयोग
CENTRAL INFORMATION COMMISSION
बाबागंगानाथमार्ग, मुनिरका
Baba Gangnath Marg, Munirka
नई दिल्ली, **New Delhi – 110067**

नितीय अपील संख्या/Second Appeal No.

CIC/EEALT/A/2017/ 165710

Shri S P Manchanda   -अपीलकर्ता/Appellant

VERSUS/बनाम

PIO, Asst. Commissioner (IMFL), O/o The Commissioner of Excise, Entt. & Luxury Tax, GNCTD, Vikas Bhawan, I.P. Estate, New Delhi. Through: Shri Lalit Mittal, Asstt. Commissioner(Excise)/PIO

...प्रतिवादी /Respondent

Through:

Shri Lalit Mittal, Asstt.

Commissioner(Excise)/PIO

Date of Hearing	:	07.06.2019
Date of Decision	:	11.7.2019
Information Commissioner:		Shri Y. K. Sinha

Relevant facts emerging from appeal:

RTI application filed on	:	14.07.2017
PIO replied on	:	14.08.2017
First Appeal filed on	:	21.08.2017
First Appellate Order on	:	25.08.2017

2nd Appeal/complaint received on:18.09.2017

Information sought and background of the case

The Appellant vide his RTI application on 14.07.2017sought information on 10points relating to the closing/shifting of the liquor shops situated in Keshav Puram residential colony near DIET/schools. The Appellant sought details of action taken on his complaint and details of inspection of the site, asking correct / exact distance of each of the liquor shops from nearby educational institutions and religious places as per Delhi Excise Rules, 2010 and matters related thereto.

Having received a dissatisfactory reply from the CPIO vide letter dated 14.08.2017, the Appellant filed first appeal on 21.08.2017. The FAA passed an Page 2 of 2order in this regard on 25.08.2017 upholding the CPIO's response. Dissatisfied, the appellant approached the Commission with his Second Appeal. Facts emerging in Course of Hearing: Both Appellant and Respondent (Shri Lalit Mittal, AC (Excise), Excise Deptt, GNCTD) are present during the hearing. The Appellant contends that the PIO of the Respondent Public Authority has provided an evasive reply and has not supplied the information desired by him. Moreover, the Appellant alleges that the First Appellate Authority did not adjudicate the First Appeal properly. On the other hand, the First Appellate Authority's Order dated 25.8.17 mentions that, "the Appellant earlier also filed RTI and appealed in this regard. The PIO has already provided the requisite information in response to his multiple RTIs. This being so, the appeals are disposed off accordingly." The PIO reiterates FAA's contention during the hearing. Decision It is apparent that the information provided to the Respondent in response to the present RTI as well

    Embrace Your Own Power to Fight Corruption

as earlier RTIs on the same subject, has not satisfied the Appellant, who has raised an issue of larger public interest. It is important that the Respondent provides specific information to allay the concerns of the Respondent, given that the issue of location of liquor shops in the vicinity of educational institutions and religious places is of public importance. The PIO should endeavor to provide a detailed and specific response to the queries raised by the Appellant in his RTI. In case the information is voluminous, the Appellant should at least be given an opportunity to inspect the records so as to allay his concerns. Notwithstanding the contention of the FAA and PIO regarding multiple RTIs filed by the Appellant, the PIO is hereby directed to provide a specific and detailed reply to the Appellant within 3 weeks, from the date of issue of this order, addressing the queries raised by the Appellant, under intimation to the Commission.

The appeal is disposed off with the above directions.

Y. K. Sinha (वाई.के.सिन्हा)
Information Commissioner (सूचनाआायुक्त)

National Pharmaceutical Pricing Authority (NPPA)

When my wife was hospitalised due to heart problem in 2015, I came to know that hospitals were making huge profits from selling cardiac stents at a price much more than import-price to treat blockages in the heart. I filed many complaints, RTI application to know the basis of fixing price of all types of cardiac stents by National Pharmaceutical Pricing Authority (NPPA). When I could not get satisfactory reply I filed an appeal to FAA and Central Information Commission (CIC) which finally led to capping the prices of stents to 1/5th the cost charged by hospitals. According to CIC decision dated 22 Feb. 2017, this success will help so many unfortunate citizens whose loved ones are in need of a cardiac stent but are not able to bear the exaggerated cost. Honourable Information Commission also appreciated my efforts for having espoused a cause of larger public interest.

Union Ministry of Health & Family Welfare

On 2017, I filed RTI-petition to NPPA seeking information regarding whether or not government was aware of some oncology medicines required for treating cancer had MRP printed which was many times more than ex-factory price or import price with much higher profit margin and if yes, steps taken by the Authority to regulate their prices and action taken agains manufacturers, importers, distributers and hospitals and doctors for looting the hapless patients. When complete reply was not furnished by PIO, I filed 1st appeal and then 2nd appeal before CIC. Serious issues such as reducing the cost of cancer medicines and generic medicines were heard by the Central Information Commission. The Information Commissioner Bimal Julka passing a significant order on 1st Oct. 2018 recommended to the Union Ministry of Health and Family Welfare, Department of Pharmaceuticals and NPPA to initiate a coordinated attempt to address the issue of checking the menace of overpricing of essential drugs and excessive trade margins to promote greater transparency for the benefit of the common man within a period of two months. This finally led to reduction of prices over 100 oncology medicines.

CONCLUSION

One evening a few months ago, my MTNL landlines suddenly went dead along with several hundred others in Keshav Puram area in Delhi. Upon investigation, it was learned that a gang of thieves had dug up and stolen underground cables worth thousands of rupees, working in broad daylight on busy roads. What a daring theft! But this theft might have been prevented, if only some passer-by had asked the fake telecom workers to show identity cards, letter of authorization for digging etc. It is likely that the thieves would have immediately fled, and many consumers of the area would have benefited. As a matter of fact, our right to information is exercised not only by filing RTI applications. It may also be exercised by going out of our way to find out why and how public works are carried out. It is every citizen's right and also a duty to become a guardian of public place and public wealth – to become an unpaid policeman. For example, a citizen sees road-digging in progress. He has a right and indeed a duty to spend 4-5 minutes understanding what is going on. He has the duty to ask questions that proves that the road-diggers are authorised. He has the right to know from public information officer of the department about the work going on and to take Xerox copies of any identification or permission that he is shown and to ask for the names of the contractors and municipal engineer responsible and to get proof of the starting and completion date of the road project along with expenditure. He also has the right to draw samples of cement-concrete mix, send them to laboratories for testing and file complaints by phone or in writing if anything is amiss.

RTI means not only the 'right to get information' but also includes the right to 'inspection of work, documents, records, taking notes, extracts or certified copies of documents, records, taking samples of materials, etc.' The RTI Act was introduced with the sole objective of empowering people, containing corruption, and bringing transparency and accountability in the working of the Government. If we do not exercise these rights given to us under RTI Act, they will always remain in theory. The RTI Act has already made a difference to the lives of many citizens. It is the duty of each and every activist to put these rights into practice for their own benefit as well as for the well-being of the society and future generations. A citizen's duty does not end with voting and the RTI Act is a great tool for citizens to come together and be more involved. The government is taking steps to make sure that citizens are not denied the right to information by making the application and follow up process easy. Most importantly, the applicant making request for the information is not under the obligation to provide any reason for requesting of his information.

Right to Information Act of India is the top 5 laws in the world.

RTI is like a 10 rupee PIL for citizens.

Use it.

     Embrace Your Own Power to Fight Corruption

CHAPTER 3

CONSUMER PROTECTION ACT, 2019

ENHANCING CONSUMER RIGHTS

Consumer refers to a person that purchases goods and services generated within the economy. Consumer protection means protecting the rights of consumers. The government has formulated laws, acts, and standardization and implementing agencies like Bureau of Indian Standards or Food Safety and Standards Act for consumer welfare but market has always stayed ahead of government initiatives and has made loopholes in the State policies. Consumers at grass root level have to be activated for their rights and get involved in various process of implementation of laws and acts, which are made for the benefit of people at large, since majority of consumers, are not aware of such acts and their rights under the law. Further appearing in consumer court does not require a lawyer, and you can represent yourself or have a relative do it for you. Moreover in a move to encourage more people to approach consumer forum/Commission, the government has proposed to bar both consumers and sellers or service providers from hiring lawyers to fight a case if the value is less than Rs.2 lakh.

Some Success Stories

Anju of New Delhi chanced upon ads of 'Personal Point' publicizing its programme for weight loss of 5 kg tummy tuck and thigh fall. She paid Rs.50,000/- and joined the programme. Her weight was 59.30 kg. But even after 3 months she weighed more, 60.50 kg as per record maintained by 'Personal Point'. Frustrated, Anju filed a complaint with Consumer Forum under Consumer Protection Act, 1986. Personal Point attributed her 'failure' to violation of instructions and irregular ending habits. But the Forum rejected this contention and ordered refund of Rs.50,000/- with interest @ 18% on the amount till date, Rs.10,000/- for mental agony and Rs,5,000/- for cost of fighting the case. It stated that Anju herself was interested in reducing weight before marriage and it was not possible that she would not follow the instructions of 'Personal Point'.

Homoeopathic doctor has no right to practice Allopathic system of medicine. In this case, the respondent, a homoeopathic doctor in Delhi, prescribed allopathic medicines for the treatment of a patient who did not respond to the medicine and subsequently died. The Supreme Court held that the right to practice the allopathic system of medicine was restricted by the Central and State Acts which prohibit such practice unless the person possesses requisite qualification and is registered according to the Acts. Based on the fact that the respondent was qualified and registered to practice Homeopathy only, he was found to be in violation of the statutory duty not to practice Allopathic system given under the section 15(3) of the Indian Medical Council Act, 1956. Respondent's act was held to be actionable negligence and he was ordered to pay a compensation of three lakh.

In Kolkata, a lady school teacher met with an accident in an OTIS elevator and rendered incapacitated for nearly 14 months at considerable loss and peace. A consumer organisation fought her case and succeeded in getting her a compensation of Rs.3,00,000/- from OTIS elevator company. It is a case of strict product and service liability. Both manufacturing and maintenance of lift was by OTIS Company. Fear of Consumer Protection Act encouraged them to settle the matter out of court.

Mr. Hitesh P. Kakadia, a student of Mahatma Gandhi Vidyamandir Dental College and Hospital, Nashik complained that he was being forced by the college principal to pay a fee of Rs.2,31,000/- while the prescribed fee as Rs.86,000/- only. A simple legal notice by a voluntary consumer organisation on behalf of the Mr. Kakadia had immediate effect and the correct fee was requested to be paid.

Justice Sinha traveled in first class from Ranchi in Patna Express. The glass shutter of the window was found broken. The rexin of the berth was torn. His wife received injury due to rusted nail in the berth. Sinha complained in the District Forum for compensation for physical and mental suffering caused in the journey. The compartment was checked under the order of the Forum and defect was confirmed by the commissioner. The state commission granted compensation for defective service.

Mr. Janardanan Madathil of Mumbai had given the passport of his wife and self to 'Make My Trip' for stamping Schangean visa after UK Visa by tour operator for the grand Europe tour. The passports were lost by 'Make My Trip' in April 2012. This resulted in police complaint and obtaining new passport incurring cost of Rs. 25000 by the consumer. Make My Trip refused to reimburse this expenditure and also did not compensate the consumers for their inability to enjoy their holiday as they could not travel in the absence of passport. A Consumer notice was sent to Make My Trip and the consumer received the reimbursement of Rs 25,000 as expenses incurred in making new passports.

Mr. Rakesh Gupta of Mumbai booked 2 return tickets to Mangalore. Due to heavy rains the consumer could not reach the airport in time and therefore called the airlines who suggested that they should pay Rs. 2000 and reschedule their tickets for other flight, which they did. Later they discovered that the previous flight was delayed by 4 hours, which was not informed to the consumer. He could have easily reached the airport to catch the delayed flight. The consumer got full refund after receiving notice from Mr. Rakesh Gupta.

Mrs. Chitra Vittal of Bangalore received a crumbled cake, bad in taste, accompanied with cheap quality greeting card cheap quality wine after a delay of two days as against her order based on the rosy photos and promises on their website, Flowersncakestoindia.com. She approached the company but the company did not respond to her complaint. When legal notice to the company, first the company started blaming the consumer that she is telling lies but the consumer soon caught the seller on wrong foot as he himself was lying that he did not receive the complaint from consumer. But soon the seller realized that he will be in lot of problems if the matter goes to the court. He refunded the consumer's full amount.

Educational institutions must refund extra fee paid. To seek

     Embrace Your Own Power to Fight Corruption

admission in a medical coaching center, the petitioner, in this case, was made to deposit a lump sum fee for two years within the first six months. When the petitioner left the course midway on account of deficiency in the services, the coaching center refused to refund the remaining amount. The State Tribunal, following the view of the apex court and the National Commission, held that no educational institution shall collect lump sum fee for the duration of the entire course and if one does, such extra fee should be returned in case the student drops out due to deficiency. It noted that any clause in a contract contrary to this is invalid due to lack of equal bargaining power and contravention of the principles of natural justice. The court was also of the opinion that additional compensation should be granted for the mental agony caused due to approaching the legal forum. However, since such was not asked in the petition, it could not be granted.

A property buyer, who invests his hard-earned money in buying a home and does not get its possession on time, not only fails to get a roof over his/her head but also ends up losing money, in the form of EMIs on the home loan and paying for a rented accommodation. Moreover, the buyer may also have to wage a long and tedious legal battle to get the justice. If possession is not delivered on time, a purchaser can send a notice to the builder, claiming refund of the amounts paid along with interest and/or damages. The buyer can also file a consumer complaint for 'deficiency in service' as defined under the Consumer Protection Act, 1986 against the builder. The flat purchaser is required to file a written complaint before the appropriate consumer dispute redressal forum set up under the act, depending on the value of the property, or the amount of damage he has suffered. Recently, Unitech was penalized Rs 3 crore by the National Consumer Dispute Redressal Commission, for delay in giving possession of its flats. In another case, in Greater Noida, more than 300 flat buyers staged a protest against a builder, for delay in giving possession. A few months ago, a developer in Mumbai was asked to compensate buyers for delay in possession.

An instance of use of the Right to Information (RTI) Act in conjunction with the Consumer Protection Act has come to notice which demonstrates how a citizen can use them for getting what he legally deserves. A railways employee, DC Sharma, had booked a flat with the Delhi Development Authority (DDA). In 2006, he sought information about the status of his flat when the DDA did not entertain his demand to mortgage the flat to the Indian Railways. He was informed that through a draw that took place on March 28, 1996, the said flat was allotted in the name of one Santosh Minhas. Claiming that he was allotted the flat after a draw that took place in 1997 following which he had deposited Rs 30,000 as registration and confirmation fee, he alleged that the flat allotted to him had also been allotted to someone else. He added that the DDA was even informed about the change in address for further correspondence regarding the allotted flat. The DDA claimed that the complainant had not deposited the demanded amount within the stipulated period up to June 18, 2000. As a result, the allotment of flat automatically stood cancelled. The district forum had upheld the argument of the DDA while a bench of the Delhi State Consumer Disputes Redressal Commission held that the demand by the DDA for confirmation amount was false and fictitious because the demand related to a flat which was non-existent. The State Commission directed the DDA to provide another flat of the same description, same condition and in the same locality or pay Rs 30.3 lakh to Sharma. Though the booking value of the flat was Rs 5,03,348, the additional amount of Rs. 24,96,652 was added because of sky rocketing prices.

   Embrace Your Own Power to Fight Corruption

After voluntary retirement from State Bank in 2007, I sought information from Reserve Bank of India (RBI) under RTI Act, 2005 about the unclaimed deposits lying in various banks and RBI guidelines to banks about repayment and the procedure how to utilize huge funds by banks. I knew that the banks submit details of unclaimed money (inoperative accounts which are more than 10 years old without claims) on yearly basis to RBI. I got to know that total of Rs.1350 crore was unclaimed funds in all scheduled banks as on 31.03.2016, which the banks were enjoying for earning profits for them. I was also informed that there was no specific policy to the banks how they should utilize the funds and that the banks were using unclaimed deposits in normal business activity i.e. lending for profit. I approached the National Consumer Disputes Redressal Commission, New Delhi for an appropriate order claiming utilization of unclaimed deposits for lending by banks being under unfair trade practices. Within few days, Reserve Bank of India issued a notification/circular dated 22.08.2008 to all public and private sector banks including foreign banks operating in India with guidelines to find the depositors or their legal heirs proactively and pay them their amount as per bank's rules. RBI also advised me that Banking Regulation Act is required to be amended for transferring the funds to Consumer Protection Fund or similar Fund. The Indian Banks Association (IBA) informed me that they are examining feasibility of creating a database to enable the customers find their deposits and claim accordingly. Reply sent by RBI and the circular issued on 20.08.2008 is reproduced in the following pages.

Unclaimed Deposits/Inoperative Accounts in banks

RBI/2008-09/138

DBOD.No.Leg. BC. 34/09.07.005/2008-09

August 22, 2008

All Scheduled Commercial Banks (Excluding RRBs)

Dear Sir,

<u>Unclaimed Deposits/Inoperative Accounts in banks</u>

1. Please refer to our Circular DBOD.No.Com.BC.109/ C.408/A-77 dated October 1, 1977 wherein banks were advised that deposit accounts which have not been operated upon over a period, say two years should be segregated and maintained in separate ledger/s. Further, banks were also advised vide our circular no. DBOD. No.Leg.BC.45/C.466 (IV)/89 dated November 15, 1989 that they should ensure that their branches follow-up accounts which remained inoperative for a year or so by sending suitable advices to the customers and if the said letters are returned undelivered, they may immediately be put on enquiry to find out the whereabouts of customers or their legal heirs in case they are deceased.

2. In view of the increase in the amount of the unclaimed deposits with banks year after year and the inherent risk

  Embrace Your Own Power to Fight Corruption

associated with such deposits, it is felt that banks should play a more pro-active role in finding the whereabouts of the account holders whose accounts have remained inoperative. Further several complaints have been received in respect of difficulties faced by the customers on account of their accounts having been classified as inoperative. Moreover, there is a feeling that banks are undeservedly enjoying the unclaimed deposits, while paying no interest on it. Keeping these factors in view, we have reviewed the above instructions issued by us and advise banks to follow the instructions detailed below while dealing with inoperative accounts:

i.   Banks should make an annual review of accounts in which there are no operations (i.e. no credit or debit other than crediting of periodic interest or debiting of service charges) for more than one year. The banks may approach the customers and inform them in writing that there has been no operation in their accounts and ascertain the reasons for the same. In case the non operation in the account is due to shifting of the customers from the locality, they may be asked to provide the details of the new bank accounts to which the balance in the existing account could be transferred.

ii.   If the letters are returned undelivered, they may immediately be put on enquiry to find out the whereabouts of customers or their legal heirs in case they are deceased.

iii. In case the whereabouts of the customers are not traceable, banks should consider contacting the persons who had introduced the account holder. They could also consider contacting the employer/ or any other person whose details are available with them. They could also consider contacting the account holder telephonically in case his telephone number/Cell number has been furnished to the bank. In case of Non Resident accounts, the bank may also contact the account holders through e-mail and obtain their confirmation of the details of the account.

iv. A savings as well as current account should be treated as inoperative/dormant if there are no transactions in the account for over a period of two years.

v. In case any reply is given by the account holder giving the reasons for not operating the account, banks should continue classifying the same as an operative account for one more year within which period the account holder may be requested to operate the account. However, in case the account holder still does not operate the same during the extended period, banks should classify the same as inoperative account after the expiry of the extended period.

vi. For the purpose of classifying an account as 'inoperative' both the type of transactions i.e. debit as well as credit transactions induced at the instance of customers as well as third party should be considered. However, the service charges levied by the bank or interest credited by the bank should not be considered.

    Embrace Your Own Power to Fight Corruption

vii.   Further, the segregation of the inoperative accounts is from the point of view of reducing risk of frauds etc. However, the customer should not be inconvenienced in any way, just because his account has been rendered inoperative. The classification is there only to bring to the attention of dealing staff, the increased risk in the account. The transaction may be monitored at a higher level both from the point of view of preventing fraud and making a Suspicious Transactions Report. However, the entire process should remain un-noticeable by the customer.

viii.   Operation in such accounts may be allowed after due diligence as per risk category of the customer. Due diligence would mean ensuring genuineness of the transaction, verification of the signature and identity etc. However, it has to be ensured that the customer is not inconvenienced as a result of extra care taken by the bank.

ix.   There should not be any charge for activation of inoperative account.

x.   Banks are also advised to ensure that the amounts lying in inoperative accounts ledger are properly audited by the internal auditors/statutory auditors of the bank.

xi.   Interest on savings bank accounts should be credited on regular basis whether the account is operative or not. If a Fixed Deposit Receipt matures and proceeds are unpaid, the amount left unclaimed with the bank will attract savings bank rate of interest.

3. Banks may also consider launching a special drive for finding the whereabouts of the customers/legal heirs in respect of existing accounts which have already been transferred to the separate ledger of 'inoperative accounts.'

Yours faithfully
(Prashant Saran)
Chief General Manager-in-Charge

CONSUMERS CAN CHEER NOW as the Consumer Protection Act, 2019 has recently replaced the three decade old Consumer Protection Act, 1986. While using the same phrase in its preamble, the 2019 Act has substantially enhanced the scope of protection afforded to consumers, by bringing within its purview advertising claims, endorsements and product liability, all of which play a fundamental role in altering consumer behavior and retail trends in the 21st century.

Set out below are some of the Key Highlights of the New Act:

Covers E-Commerce Transactions: The New Act has widened the definition of 'consumer'. The definition now includes any

    Embrace Your Own Power to Fight Corruption

person who buys any goods, whether through offline or online transactions, electronic means, teleshopping, direct selling or multi-level marketing. The earlier Act did not specifically include e-commerce transactions, and this lacuna has been addressed by the New Act.

Enhancement of Pecuniary Jurisdiction: Revised pecuniary limits have been fixed under the New Act. Accordingly, the district forum can now entertain consumer complaints where the value of goods or services paid does not exceed Rs.1,00,00,000 (Rupees one crore). The State Commission can entertain disputes where such value exceeds Rs. 1,00,00,000 (Rupees one crore) but does not exceed Rs.10,00,00,000 (Rupees ten crore), and the National Commission can exercise jurisdiction where such value exceeds Rs. 10,00,00,000 (Rs. ten crore).

E-Filing of Complaints: The New Act provides flexibility to the consumer to file complaints with the jurisdictional consumer forum located at the place of residence or work of the consumer. This is unlike the current practice of filing it at the place of purchase or where the seller has its registered office address. The New Act also contains enabling provisions for consumers to file complaints electronically and for hearing and/or examining parties through video-conferencing. This is aimed to provide procedural ease and reduce inconvenience and harassment for the consumers.

Establishment of Central Consumer Protection Authority: The New Act proposes the establishment of a regulatory authority known as the Central Consumer Protection Authority (CCPA), with wide powers of enforcement. The CCPA will have an investigation wing, headed by a Director-General, which may conduct inquiry or investigation into consumer law violations. The

CCPA has been granted wide powers to take sue-motto actions, recall products, order reimbursement of the price of goods/ services, cancel licenses and file class action suits, if a consumer complaint affects more than 1 (one) individual.

Product Liability & Penal Consequences: The New Act has introduced the concept of product liability and brings within its scope, the product manufacturer, product service provider and product seller, for any claim for compensation. The term 'product seller' is defined to include a person who is involved in placing the product for a commercial purpose and as such would include e-commerce platforms as well. The defense that e-commerce platforms merely act as 'platforms' or 'aggregators' will not be accepted. There are increased liability risks for manufacturers as compared to product service providers and product sellers, considering that under the New Act, manufacturers will be liable in product liability action even where he proves that he was not negligent or fraudulent in making the express warranty of a product. Certain exceptions have been provided under the New Act from liability claims, such as, that the product seller will not be liable where the product has been misused, altered or modified.

Unfair Trade Practices: The New Act introduces a specific broad definition of Unfair Trade Practices, which also includes sharing of personal information given by the consumer in confidence, unless such disclosure is made in accordance with the provisions of any other law.

Penalties for Misleading Advertisement: The CCPA may impose a penalty of up to INR 1,000,000 (Indian Rupees One Million) on a manufacturer or an endorser, for a false or misleading advertisement. The CCPA may also sentence them to imprisonment for up to 2 (two) years for the same. In case of a

    Embrace Your Own Power to Fight Corruption

subsequent offence, the fine may extend to INR 5,000,000 (Indian Rupees Five Million) and imprisonment of up to 5 (five) years. The CCPA can also prohibit the endorser of a misleading advertisement from endorsing that particular product or service for a period of up to 1 (one) year. For every subsequent offence, the period of prohibition may extend to 3 (three) years. The New Act fixes liability on endorsers considering that there have been numerous instances in the recent past where consumers have fallen prey to unfair trade practices under the influence of celebrities acting as brand ambassadors. In such cases, it becomes important for the endorser to take the onus and exercise due diligence to verify the veracity of the claims made in the advertisement to refute liability claims.

Provision for Alternate Dispute Resolution: The New Act provides for mediation as an Alternate Dispute Resolution mechanism, making the process of dispute adjudication simpler and quicker. This will help with the speedier resolution of disputes and reduce pressure on consumer courts, which already have numerous cases pending before them.

There were a total of 6 consumer rights which have been defined in the Consumer Protection Bill, and those are:

- Right to Safety
- Right to be Informed
- Right to Choose
- Right to be Heard
- Right to Seek Redressal
- Right to Consumer Education

So, now in addition to the existing consumer rights, there are 5 new consumer rights you get as a consumer in this 2019 Act.

1. **Right to file a complaint from anywhere:** According to this new right, consumers can now file a complaint with the District Consumer Commission or State Consumer Commission from anywhere, home, office or while on a weekend trip. Presently, the consumers are required to file a case only at the place where the product was purchased or where the seller of the product has his registered office. The consumer affairs ministry will now frame rules for electronic filing of complaints and specify norms for paying the required fee digitally. This will reduce harassment of consumers to a great extent.

2. **Right to seek compensation under product liability:** Any complainant can file a case against the manufacturer or seller of a product for any loss caused to the complainant on account of a defective product, which applies to all services. If there is a manufacturing defect or the product in question does not conform to the express warranty the manufacturer or the seller will be held liable. This provision brings e-commerce under its ambit.

3. **Right to protect consumers as a class:** If you have a complaint that relates to violation of consumer rights or unfair trade practices or misleading advertisements that are prejudicial to the interests of consumers as a class, you can forward the complaint in writing or in electronic mode to district collector or the commissioner of regional office or the Central Consumer Protection Authority (CCPA) for class action.

4. **Right to seek a hearing using video conferencing:** According to this, any complaint will be presented before the district commission based on an affidavit and

   Embrace Your Own Power to Fight Corruption

documentary evidence placed before it. If an application has been forwarded by a consumer for hearing through video conference, the commission can allow for this provision.

5. **Right to know why a complaint was rejected:** No commission can reject a complaint without hearing the complainant. The commission, in fact, must decide about admitting or rejecting a complaint within 21 days, by which if it is not decided then the complaint is deemed as having been admitted.

    With the New Act all set to become the law, gone are the days, where the 'consumer was asked to beware'. A consumer is now the one who assumes to be treated like a King. Hence, it is important for consumer driven businesses (such as, retail, e-commerce) to be mindful of the changes in the legal landscape and have robust policies dealing with consumer redressal in place. Consumer driven businesses must also strive to take extra precautions against unfair trade practices and unethical business practices.

Solving Consumer Problems

Disappointed by a product or service you've paid for? You don't have to settle for shabby performance. Most businesses want to keep you happy so you'll keep coming back. These strategies and **our sample complaint letter** can help.

Return to the Store or Website

You can solve many consumer problems by talking to a store employee, or if you bought the item online, by returning to the website. Do this as soon as possible because some retailers have time limits on returns and refunds.

Online retailers should provide return instructions on the site or on your receipt. When shopping online, it's wise to consider the company's reputation and return policy before you buy. If the employee doesn't have the authority to help you, ask for a supervisor or manager. With each person, calmly and accurately explain the problem and what you would like them to do. Keep a record of your conversations—who you spoke with and when, and what action they promised.

Call Customer Service

You may need to speak to someone at the company's national headquarters or to the manufacturer of the product. Many companies provide a toll—free number or address for their customer service department on the product packaging, warranty, or receipt. If the first person you speak to can't help, ask for a supervisor.

Use Social Media

Social media offers an alternative to filing a formal consumer complaint. Many companies have people to monitor posts and complaints about their service on social media pages. Your post will be most effective if you use a reasonable tone and explain the problem clearly. To avoid negative perceptions, the company may respond quickly to your problem. While there is no guarantee, it's worth a try.

Write a Complaint Letter

If a call doesn't work, use this sample letter and these tips to draft an effective complaint:

- Be clear and concise. Describe the item you bought and the problem, include serial or model numbers, and the name and location of the seller.

- State exactly what you want done and how long you are willing to wait for a response. Be reasonable.

- Don't write an angry, sarcastic, or threatening letter. The person reading your letter probably isn't responsible for the problem, but may be very helpful in resolving it.

- Include copies of relevant documents, like receipts, repair orders, and warranties. Keep the originals.

- Provide your name, address, and phone numbers. If an account is involved, be sure to include the account number.

You may want to send your letter by certified mail and request a return receipt. You'll have proof that the company got your letter and who signed for it.

Use this sample to draft a complaint letter about a product or service.

[Your Address]

[Your City, State, PIN Code]

[Date]

[Name of Contact Person]

[Title]

[Shop/Company Name]

[Street Address]

[City, State, PIN Code]

Dear [Contact Person]:

On [date], I bought [or had repaired] a [name of the product with the serial or model number or service performed]. I made this purchase at [location, date, and other important details of the transaction].

Unfortunately, your product has not performed well [or the service was inadequate] because [state the problem].

To resolve the problem, I would appreciate your [state the specific action you want]. Enclosed are copies [copies, not originals] of my records [receipts, guarantees, warranties, cancelled checks, contracts, model and serial numbers, and any other documents] concerning this purchase/repair.

I look forward to your reply and a resolution to my problem. I will wait [set a time limit] before seeking third-party assistance. Please contact me at the above address or by phone [home or office numbers with area codes].

Sincerely,

[Your Name]

However, If the complaint is not resolved by above methods, you may file consumer complaint and appear before the consumer court without the assistance of lawyer or advocate.

TIPS ON SUGGESTED CONSUMER COURT COMPLAINT FORMAT

Before The Consumer Disputes Redressal Forum/Commission
Complaint No_______________________of

In the Matter of:

(Name and address of the complainant) Complainant Versus
(Name and address of the opposite party) Opposite Party

COMPLAINT UNDER SECTION 12 OF THE CONSUMER PROTECTION ACT

Most Respectfully Submitted as Under:

1. That the complainant is a consumer within the definition of the Consumer Protection Act and is constrained to approach this Forum against the gross acts of the opposite party wherein he has committed serious deficiency of services and unfair trade practices.

2. That the brief facts leading to the filing of the present complaint are as under:

(Narrate the brief facts of the matter)

3. That the supportive documents in above are as under:

(Enclose all the documents in support)

4. That the aforesaid amounts to deficiency in services and unfair trade practice and the Complainant is entitled to refund of his entire amount of money paid to the opposite party. The Complainant is also entitled to a compensation of Rs. .... against the aforesaid deficiency of services by the Opposite party as the Complainant has been made to suffer due to the above said acts of the opposite party. The Complainant is also entitled to compensation in lieu of physical pain, mental agony, and trauma due to all this.

PRAYER

It is, therefore, prayed that the Court may direct the opposite party to refund the entire amount paid to him along with interest at the market rate along with an amount of Rs. .... as compensation to the Complainant. That the Complainant is also entitled to the cost of the present litigation. Any other order as the Hon'ble Court may deem fit and proper in the facts and circumstances in favour of the Complainant be passed.

COMPLAINANT/Name & Mobile No.

***

Assert Your Rights as a Consumer
An Aware Consumer is an Asset to the Nation

CHAPTER 4

PUBLIC INTEREST LITIGATION

A POWERFUL TOOL TO FIX THE SYSTEM

Are you disappointed with the decisions of government and the policies it is implementing? Do you think the decisions by the government are causing the violation of rules and regulations or fundamental human rights, helping black money circulation and corruption, doing social injustice, etc.? Are you interested in changing these things and fix the system through law? If yes, then public interest litigation (PIL) is for you. In recent years, many PIL petitions are being filed. Regardless of winning or losing they are creating awareness of issues and making an impact on the lives of the people. Any individual or a group of people can file for a PIL if they prove to the court that they are not filing the petition for their personal agenda. A PIL may be filed against state government, central government, municipal authority not any private party.

In Indian law, public interest litigation means litigation for the protection of the public interest. In simple terms, a PIL is a petition that an individual or a non-government organisation or citizen groups, can file in the court seeking justice in an issue that has a larger public interest. It aims at giving common people an access to the judiciary to obtain legal redress for a greater cause. PIL is a case filed by any individual against any activity which can harm or damage interest of public or society as a whole. In PIL, the right to file suit is given to a member of the public by the courts through judicial activism. Any public spirited citizen, whether he is an advocate or lawyer or a common man like me can move/approach the court for the public cause (in the interests of the public or public welfare) by filing a PIL petition.

With regard to filing of a PIL, there is no statutory procedure of filing a PIL, but it has to be filed in a similar way as that of writs. A PIL can be even in the form of letters or telegrams to the Chief Justice of Supreme Court or High Court directly or through the PIL lawyer. A PIL to be filed should be filed under Article 226 of Indian Constitution, if it is being filed before High Court and under Article 32, if it is filed before the Hon'ble Supreme Court. The court fee for filing PIL is generally Rs.50 per petitioner/ respondent. Plus, the expenses on documentation (printing, photocopying, conveyance etc.) would have to be incurred, which are generally in the range of a few thousand rupees. PIL can be filed either in High Court or Supreme Court depending on the situation. Both the courts have power to entertain the public interest litigation.

Before filing a PIL one has to do the complete research about the issue. When a PIL is filed concerning many people, the petitioner needs to consult all the individuals and groups which are affected. Once you are sure of filing a PIL, collect all the vital information and documents as evidence to support your case. You can argue the case on your own or appoint a lawyer to argue on behalf of you. It is always advisable to consult a lawyer before filing the PIL. If you are interested in arguing the case on your own then be prepared to explain the problem and convince the court in the time you have been allotted. Once the PIL copy is ready to be filed in the High Court, then submit two copies of the petition to the court. Along with this, one copy of the petition needs to be served to the respondents in advance. This proof of serving the petition copy to the respondents has to be affixed in the petition. If the PIL is filed in the Supreme Court, then five copies of petition need to be submitted to the court. Respondent is served with the petition copy when the court issues the notice regarding the same.

For socially conscious citizens who would like to fix the system through a court of law, PIL is a powerful tool. Although I am not an advocate or lawyer, I have filed many PILs in the High Court of Delhi on various issues; some of them are exhibited in the following pages.

Rationalise Circle Rates in Delhi to Curb Corruption

Circle rates of immovable properties in Delhi/New-Delhi are highly irrational, unrealistic and arbitrarily fixed, as a result

   Embrace Your Own Power to Fight Corruption

there is generation of black money in some areas where circle rates are much lower than current market rates and on the other hand there are no buyers of properties/flats where circle rates are too high, as stamp duty is generally paid on circle rate notified by the government. These circle rates were first notified in 2007 and revised 4 times after that, last revision was done in September 2014. After complaints were filed by the public to rationalise circle rates, a committee was constituted on 6th Feb 2014 by Govt of NCT of Delhi under the chairmanship of DM (West) Revenue Department for the 4th revision of circle rates and it submitted its report in March 2014. The Expert Committee also accepted anomalies in circle rates and expressed its concern on black money and loss of revenue due to illogical circle rates. This report was uploaded on website of the department as per Hon'ble CIC order. Despite committee report to rationalise circle rates, Delhi Govt on 22 Sept 2014 arbitrarily increased circle rates of land, cost of construction and built-up flats by 20-percent flat in all categories of location throughout Delhi without application of mind and without considering recommendation of the committee resulting very high circle rates in some areas.

It is surprising that while circle rates of Land in Delhi vary widely from Rs.774,000 per sq. meter in 'A' category of location to only Rs.23,280 per sq. meter in 'H' category, circle rates of Flats built on the same land are uniform throughout the city. Thus Circle rate of a LIG flat in backward area, Narela (category G) is same (Rs.36.92 lacs) akin to LIG flat located in posh colony, Vasant Kunj (category C). It is significant to note here that circle rates of Flats as notified by another government agency in Delhi, Municipal Corporation of Delhi (MCD) vary widely from Rs.40,000 per sq. mtr. in backward colony (Category H) to Rs.5,00,000 per sq.

meter in posh colony (Category A) for the purpose of charging property tax. Further, an another government agency in Delhi, Delhi Development Authority (DDA) also sells flats in different areas of Delhi/New Delhi at different rates depending upon the infrastructure facilities in those areas. Since circle rates of Flats as notified by revenue department of Govt of NCT of Delhi are uniform across Delhi, stamp duty charged on same-area flats is also identical throughout Delhi whether the flat is located in backward area in G/H category e.g. Narela, Bawana or in posh colony in A/B category e.g. Vasant Kunj, Munirka. As a result, circle rate in backward colonies/areas is much higher than current market value of flats and Govt is (illegally) charging much-higher stamp duty on each sale/purchase transaction. On the other hand in posh colonies, circle rate of similar flat is much lower than market rate of flats and the purchaser is happy to pay lower stamp duty on the basis of (lower) circle rates, the rest is paid in black. Furthermore in backward areas where the government circle rate is high, nobody is willing to pay unjustified higher stamp duty to buy a flat and Govt is again losing revenue by way of stamp duty and registration charges. It is also important to mention here that if a buyer is interested to purchase the property through bank loan at current market value which is lower than circle rate value, he is required to pay bribe to get documents completed at the consideration (bank-loan) amount, although he is forced to pay stamp duty on circle rate. More importantly, the Income Tax Department is now constrained to treat every buyer of property here, as a crook and a dishonest person. The officers per force must charge tax at 30-percent on the difference between the stamp duty value (circle rate) and the actual price of property i.e. on market value treating it as the application of his unaccounted income. Likewise, the

   Embrace Your Own Power to Fight Corruption

seller is also slammed with additional tax liability on assumed long term capital gains calculated on the basis of circle rate. As a result of all this, grave hardship and harassment is being caused to the residents of the many areas with the result purchase and sale of properties have virtually stopped in many parts of the city. The residents of New Friends colony and Narela-flats are caught in an unprecedented hopeless and harrowing situation from which they have no recourse. The hardship and trauma suffered by the property owners, majority of whom are retired and very senior citizens is grave and very real. The residents are being denied their fundamental rights to sell and buy property and pay stamp duty at market rates. It is just like you buy a product at Rs.1 lakh but asked to pay GST on Rs.3 lakh.

A PIL WP(C) 6607/2013 was filed by me in person in 2003 against irrational circle rates with prayer to the High Court of Delhi to direct Govt of NCT of Delhi to rationalise circle rates of properties which was disposed of by the court to be treated by the respondent as a representation and to be disposed of by a speaking order as expeditiously as possible. When nothing happened and government took no action in next 6 years, I again filed PIL WP(C) 5185/2019 in Delhi High Court for justice in larger public interest. On 3.9.2019 the Chief Justice of the court issued notice to the government and next date of hearing was fixed as 27.11.2019. On this date I appeared in the court as petitioner-in-person and pleaded for relief. Hon'ble High Court of Delhi disposed of my petition stating that it is a complex issue and the government has constituted a committee for calculation and revision of circle rates on scientific basis.

For further information, order issued by the HC is available in the following pages.

IN THE HIGH COURT OF DELHI AT NEW DELHI
W.P.(C) 5185/2019

S.P. MANCHANDA..... Petitioner

Through: Petitioner in person.

Versus

GOVT. OF NCT OF DELHI..... Respondent

Through: Ms. Zubeda Begum, Adv. with Ms. Sana Ansari, Adv.

CORAM:

HON'BLE THE CHIEF JUSTICE
HON'BLE MR. JUSTICE MANMOHAN
ORDER
24.10.2013

After some arguments, the petitioner who appears in person prays that the present writ petition be treated as a representation to the Government of NCT of Delhi who should be directed to dispose of the same as expeditiously as possible. Keeping in view the aforesaid prayer, the present petition is directed to be treated by the respondent as a representation and to be disposed of by a speaking order as expeditiously as possible. With the aforesaid directions, the writ petition is disposed of. CHIEF JUSTICE

MANMOHAN, J

OCTOBER 24, 2013/

   Embrace Your Own Power to Fight Corruption

IN THE HIGH COURT OF DELHI AT NEW DELHI
W.P.(C) 5185/2019

SURAJ PARKASH MANCHANDA..... Petitioner

Through: Petitioner in person.

Versus

GOVT. OF NCT OF DELHI..... Respondent

Through: Mr. Chirayu Jain, Adv. for

Mr.Ramesh Singh, Standing Counsel

for GNCTD.

CORAM:

HON'BLE THE CHIEF JUSTICE

HON'BLE MR. JUSTICE ANUP JAIRAM BHAMBHANI

O R D E R

%14.05.2019

Issue notice.

Mr. Chirayu Jain, Advocate appears and accepts notice on behalf of GNCTD.

Counter-affidavit be filed within four weeks. Rejoinder thereto, if any, be filed within two weeks thereafter.

List on 03rd September, 2019.

CHIEF JUSTICE

ANUP JAIRAM BHAMBHANI, J.

MAY 14, 2019/uj

IN THE HIGH COURT OF DELHI AT NEW DELHI
W.P.(C) 5185/2019

SURAJ PARKASH MANCHANDA..... Petitioner

Through: Petitioner-in-person.

Versus

GOVT. OF NCT OF DELHI ..... Respondent

Through: Mr. Ramesh Singh, SC, GNCTD with

Mr. Chirayu Jain & Mr. Ishan

Agrawal, Advs. for GNCTD.

CORAM:

HON'BLE THE CHIEF JUSTICE
HON'BLE MR. JUSTICE C.HARI SHANKAR
O R D E R
% 03.09.2019

Counsel appearing for the respondent submitted that affidavit of Principal Secretary (Revenue) shall be filed. He submitted that new circle rates are already going to be finalized by the respondent as early as possible on a scientific basis.

Petitioner, who appears in person, submitted that there cannot be the same circle rate in the most posh area of the city of Delhi and in other areas of the city of Delhi. Few examples are also given which are enumerated at Page 119 of the writ petition which is a report given by the Expert Committee. Petitioner also submitted that because of arbitrarily fixed circle rates either there will be under-valuation or over-valuation of the properties which may result in loss of revenue or generation of the litigation in the Courts.

Time as prayed for is granted to the counsel for the respondent to file an affidavit on or before the next date of hearing.

List on 27.11.2019.

CHIEF JUSTICE

     Embrace Your Own Power to Fight Corruption

Language of Delhi High Court and Supreme Court is English only!

Legal system exists for litigants. It is the right of every litigant to fight case without hiring any lawyer. However, according to existing provision rules, most of the litigants residing in Delhi who are incapable of speaking English are being deprived of this right in the High Court of Delhi. Any one of these residents of Delhi is forced to hire an English knowing lawyer if he or she files any case in this court or if somebody files any case against him or her in this court, whereas it is the right of every individual to fight case without hiring any lawyer. Even if somebody hires an English knowing lawyer, he or she may not be able to understand whether the lawyer is presenting the important points about the case or not. While it is true that the person seeking justice cannot be driven out of the Court on account of language, it is also equally true that an officer of the Court is equally expected to honour the mother tongue or language of the litigant or the under-trial and also the primary official language of the State. Just like dispensation of justice is the prime concern and duty of the Court, language should not come in any way of dispensation of justice. It ought to be the effort of legislative that justice is accessible to all and not to be prerogative of a select few elite English speaking people.

In August 2014, Director General (Prisons) at Central Jail Tihar at Delhi also sent a representation to Delhi High Court and highlighted overcrowding problem particularly those of under-trials mentioning their inability to understand the proceedings of trial in various courts in Delhi as it is conducted only in English language. The representation further pointed out that these under-trials have to just stand as mute spectators to the trial proceedings whenever witness is being examined and the matter is being argued. Many of these under-trials have requested jail authorities for conduct of trial in Hindi language as they will be able to understand and appreciate the trial proceedings which in turn will also help in expeditious disposal of their cases.

Although Article 343 (1) of the Constitutional says that language of Supreme Court of India and High Courts in various states will be English only, Article 343(2) states that the Governor of the state, with the consent of President of India may introduce state language in the high court of that state. High courts of Rajasthan, Bihar, U.P. and M.P. already have proceedings in Hindi language also. So Hindi language should not be banned or prohibited in Delhi High Court in Delhi state which has Hindi its first official language and in which state capital most of the people speak and understand Hindi.

A PIL WP(C) 1781/2014 was filed by me in person as trustee of Prakash India with relief sought for directions to permit optional use of Hindi language in pleadings and proceedings in the District Courts as well as High Court. The respondent of the High Court stated that it is pending consideration on the administrative side. Learned counsel for the respondents further stated that the same would be considered and the decision communicated to the petitioner. Although my petition was not considered at that time, litigants are now easily permitted/allowed to speak/pleading in Hindi language also.

IN THE HIGH COURT OF DELHI AT NEW DELHI
W.P. (C) 1781/2014

CM APPL.3717/2014

PRAKASH INDIA ..... Petitioner

Through: Mr. Rabin Majumdar, Advocate.

Versus

HIGH COURT OF DELHI and ANR ..... Respondents

Through: Mr. RajshekharRao, Advocate for R-1/DHC.

Ms. RuchiSindhwani, Additional Standing Counsel, GNCTD with Ms. Bandana

Shukla and Ms. MeghaBharara, Advocates for R-2.

CORAM:

HON'BLE MR. JUSTICE S. RAVINDRA BHAT
HON'BLE MR. JUSTICE R.V.EASWAR
O R D E R
25.03.2014

It is stated that the relief sought for directions to permit optional use of Hindi language in pleadings and proceedings in the District Courts as well as this Court, is pending consideration on the administrative side. Learned counsel for the respondents states that the same would be considered and the decision communicated to the petitioner.

In the light of this statement, the writ petition is disposed of along with the pending application reserving liberty to the petitioner to approach this Court at a later date if found necessary.

S. RAVINDRA BHAT, J
R.V.EASWAR, J

MARCH 25, 2014/vks/

$ 30

Long Summer Vacation in Supreme Court and Delhi High Court

Long summer vacations in Supreme Court and High courts of states were designed by erstwhile British rulers to save British judges in India from severe hot weather of this country and also to facilitate them to visit their homeland in England during summers when there were not even fans or coolers. This costly facility unfortunately continues in free India seventy years of independence even after provision of ACs in courts, homes and even in cars, that too with huge number (about 3 crores) of pendency of court-cases. Long-pending recommendation of Law Commission for reducing long court-vacations is being ignored.

A grievance-petition was sent to Union Ministry of Law and Justice to immediately scarp any privileged vacations for courts ensuring a common pattern of holidays from Supreme Court to all high courts and lower courts. Instead of closing work at courts altogether for long court-vacations, judges can be given vacations by rotation like exists system for Professors at medical colleges and Police force in government. Even lawyers desiring long vacations should not have any difficulty because they are still at liberty to seek adjourned-dates according to their convenience.

Supreme Court calendar shows week-long vacations each for Holi, Dussehra, Muharram and Diwali apart from fortnight-long winter-vacations for Christmas Day and New Year, in addition to 50 days summer vacations in May-June. If all other sections of society have no such facility of long festival-breaks and summer-vacations, it is unjustified for Supreme Court and other courts to have such a privilege.

     Embrace Your Own Power to Fight Corruption

A PIL WP(C) 4138/2013 was filed by me as Trustee of Prakash India in 2013 in the High Court of Delhi against long summer vacations in courts to curtail holidays so that pendency of litigations is reduced. The Chief Justice vide its order on 3.7.2013 stated that it is neither practically feasible nor it is advisable to have Benches sitting in rotation and that Judges do not spend their entire vacations vacationing but spend a substantial part of the time either in their office at home or in the High Court writing judgments which have been reserved by them prior to vacations. The news regarding this flimsy judgment was published next day in 16 newspapers.

IN THE HIGH COURT OF DELHI AT NEW DELHI
W.P.(C) 4138/2013

PRAKASH-INDIA ..... Petitioner

Through: Petitioner in person.

Versus

HIGH COURT OF DELHI ..... Respondent

Through: Mr Rajiv Bansal and Ms Rupali Kapoor, Advocates.

CORAM:

HON'BLE MR. JUSTICE BADAR DURREZ AHMED, ACJ
HON'BLE MR. JUSTICE VIBHU BAKHRU

ORDER

03.07.2013

This writ petition has been filed seeking a mandamus for discontinuation of the summer vacations in the High Court of Delhi. The petition also seeks quashing of the circular issued by the Registrar General notifying the summer vacations in the High Court of Delhi from June 01 to June 29, 2013. A further direction has been sought for curtailing the vacations in the High Court of Delhi by 10 to 15 days.We have heard the petitioner in person. Insofar as the quashing of the circular is concerned, that issue no longer survives inasmuch as the vacations are over and the new session has started from 01.07.2013. As regards curtailing the summer vacations of the High Court of Delhi is concerned, it is well known that the High Court has to maintain 210 court sitting days in a year and that is being religiously maintained. Moreover, the Court also functions on all Saturdays which are not otherwise declared as holidays. Apart from this, the suggestion of discontinuation of summer vacations is not practically feasible. The Judges as well as the lawyers of the Court are already over worked and they cannot be required to work anymore than what they are already doing. Perhaps, the petitioner does not know that even during the summer vacations, the High Court is not closed for those in need of urgent orders. The Vacation Benches of this Court work on Mondays, Wednesdays and Fridays during the summer vacations. Furthermore, the petitioner also does not seem to be aware of the fact that most Judges do not spend their entire vacations vacationing but spend a substantial part of the time either in their office at home or in the High Court writing judgments which have been reserved by them prior to vacations. The petitioner has also suggested that vacations may be taken on a rotation basis as is done in some police organisations and hospitals.

Unfortunately, the petitioner does not realise that those organisations cannot be compared with the Court system. It is neither practically feasible nor it is advisable to have Benches sitting in rotation. If that were to be implemented, the position insofar as the litigants are concerned might become absolutely chaotic. For all these reasons, we do not see any merit in this petition. The writ petition is dismissed.

ACTING CHIEF JUSTICE
VIBHU BAKHRU, J

JULY 03, 2013
MK

 Embrace Your Own Power to Fight Corruption

CHAPTER 5

MEDIA PUBLICATION
MOTIVATION FOR GOOD WORK

**"If you don't show appreciation to those who deserve it,
they will learn to stop doing the things you appreciate"**

When you are doing social work and get positive response from society, you are appreciated not only by the people you serve but also by media for doing well in larger public interest. Like everyone else - Acknowledgement and Appreciation is one of my greatest emotional needs. Appreciation that I received from my near & dears and acknowledgement of my work in media made me stand strong with my efforts and continue my journey with greater enthusiasm to a better future.

Media mentions were quite special to me because it made me believe three things:

1. What I am doing is of great importance

2. With so much attention, issue may eventually see a
   resolution

3. Vide coverage to masses is helping me inspire people I
   don't even know

There have been times when my RTI application for rationalisation of circle rates to curb corruption was acknowledged as "one of the best applications towards fulfillment of objectives of RTI Act" publicly by Central Information Commission (CIC) and other times when Information Commissioner while issuing order on slashing price of cardiac stents appreciated me for having espoused a cause of larger public interest. More importantly, the issue raised by me before the Hon'ble High Court of Delhi to restrict summer vacations in higher judiciary got covered in more than 16 national newspapers. I have added some of them in the book for your leisurely read.

Embrace Your own Power to Fight Corruption

by Buzzigar, August, 2017

Nearly 12 years ago, Right to Information act (RTI) was passed in the parliament and became an official law on 12th October 2005. Yet, even after a decade, a massive majority of Indians seem to widely underestimate its true potential and power. Thankfully, few RTI activists across our country have been utilizing this right in the last decade and making many small changes happen on the ground level for the betterment of our livelihood. One such activist is Suraj Prakash Manchanda from New Delhi.

Video:https://www.youtube.com/watch?v=Eh2SSF9Umkk

After retiring from a public sector bank in 2007, he discovered RTI for the first time and spent months researching more on the act and methods to use to effectively. His first success came, when he filed an RTI-application asking information about short reimbursement that he was duped out of by the bank. He sought to know the name of the officer and calculation sheet for payment of the bill. This resulted in the bank giving him the entire amount within a short time.

After that, he dedicated his life to studying RTI Act, providing public service and raising awareness about the power of RTI. He filed several RTI-petitions to various public authorities including

Prime Minister's office, Chief Minister's office, Reserve Bank of India, State Bank of India, Municipal Corporation of Delhi, Income Tax offices, Delhi Development Authority, Medical Council of India, Delhi Pollution Control Committee and Passport offices related to tax issues, incomplete construction work, pollution, situation of stray animals and several other factors that directly affected lives of people in the city.

RIGHT TO INFORMATION

Many of those RTIs led to overwhelmingly positive outcomes with the authorities promptly taking due action in interest of general public, out of the fear of information about their incompetence coming out in public. Many of the construction and public service projects that were stagnated and stalled, were resolved shortly after RTIs were filed asking details about those projects and their presumed date of completion.

In 2009, he unfortunately lost his daughter due to medical negligence after a c-section delivery in a reputed hospital in New Delhi, which led to him filing several complaints and RTI requests to Medical Council of India about the case of negligence he was pursuing, and then further appealed to Central Information Commission (CIC) after there was no proper response. All this effort finally led to the negligent doctor getting barred from practicing medicine for 3 years.

   Embrace Your Own Power to Fight Corruption

Circle rates of immovable properties in Delhi are highly illogical and arbitrarily fixed because of which there is rampant corruption and black money circulation in the capital of India. Mr. Manchanda filed grievance with the Chief Minister of Delhi and also gave suggestions to set right the situation. He also sent RTI-application to know the status of his complaint. When there was no response, he appealed to higher authority and then to CIC for seeking complete information about the action taken on his application to curb corruption. In a decision delivered in January 2015, CIC adjudged his RTI-application as one of the best applications in public interestand ordered revenue department to provide inspection of all files which the SDM wanted to conceal. He further ordered to put up report of committee on the government website.

In 2015, his wife suffered from a heart attack and was taken for a treatment in a Paschim Vihar hospital, he came to know about the hospitals making enormous revenues from selling cardiac stents at a price much more than reasonable price to treat blockage in the heart. He filed several complaints, grievance-petitions, RTIs and appeals to CIC which finally led to National Pharmaceutical Pricing Authority (NPPA) to cap the prices of stentsto 1/5th the cost charged by hospitals.

According to his decision dated 22 Feb.2017, the Information Commission Mr. Yashovardhan Azad appreciated Mr. Suraj Parkash Manchanda for having espoused a cause of larger public interest. His success will help so many unfortunate citizens whose loved ones are in need of a stent but are not able to bear the unjustified huge cost that was previously charged by the hospitals.

RTI means not only the 'right to get information' but also includes the right to 'inspection of work, documents, records, taking notes, extracts or certified copies of documents, records, taking samples of materials, etc.' If we do not exercise these rights given to us under RTI Act, they will always remain in theory. The RTI Act has already made a difference to the lives of many citizens. It is the duty of each and every individual to put these rights into practice for their own benefit as well as for the well-being of the society and our future generations.

THE ECONOMIC TIMES

CIC pitches for ban on junk food near Delhi schools.

The transparency watchdog took a grim view of junk food and colas being sold around schools and termed them "a health hazard."

By

NIDHI SHARMA

ET Bureau|

Updated: Aug 19, 2017, 01.12 AM IST

According to sources, the commission stopped short of ordering the Delhi government because it does not have the mandate to do so.

NEW DELHI: The Central Information Commission has asked the Delhi government to consider banning the sale of junk food and colas near schools in the capital, following a query by an applicant under the Right to Information (RTI) Act.

The transparency watchdog took a grim view of junk food and colas being sold around schools and termed them "a health hazard."

Information Commissioner Yashovardhan Azad passed an order asking the Delhi government to consider banning the sale of these items around schools. The commission took serious note of the issue and even directed that the order be marked to Delhi chief secretary, who was not party to the matter.

Azad acted on an appeal by SP Manchanda, a resident of Keshav Puram in north-west Delhi, who sought information on action taken by the Delhi government to ban or restrict the sale of junk food and fizzy drinks in the capital and steps taken to publicise their health hazards.

Manchanda, who submitted the RTI application in February, did not get a response and filed an appeal with the CIC in April.

"The query raised by the appellant addresses public interest, particularly the health of the children, which is at a high risk considering that the target consumer for these products are the children," Azad said in his order.

He noted that the Delhi government was not doing enough to restrict the sale of junk food. "As is well known, unfortunately, enough measures are not being taken to address this menace posing threat to public health."

Azad said the Delhi government needs to consider the matter of restricting or even banning the sale of junk food around schools.

According to sources, the commission stopped short of ordering the Delhi government because it does not have the mandate to do so.

It can only consider whether information maintained by the government has been provided under the RTI Act.

ET View: Hold Delhi Govt Accountable

The Delhi government must act swiftly to ensure a ban on the sale of cola and junk food near schools. Action should be taken against those violating the norms. It should also reach out to the central health and human resources development ministries, municipal authorities, and community groups to increase awareness of the health hazards posed by junk food. Schools too must be part of this effort. The Delhi government should be held accountable for any failure to adhere to norms.

***

THE FINANCIAL EXPRESS

Poor land valuation resulting in black money in Delhi: CIC

By: PTI

New Delhi | Published: January 11, 2015 4:13:19 PM

Difference in real value of land and circle rates in the national capital is not only facilitating black money inflow in the property market...

Difference in real value of land and circle rates in the national capital is not only facilitating black money inflow in the property market but also causing revenue loss to the exchequer, the Central Information Commission has said.

It has also directed the Chief Secretary to review the policy and carry out an inquiry.

Using its powers under the RTI Act, Information Commissioner Sridhar Acharyulu directed the Chief Secretary to have "serious look" at the policy of circle rates and put them on the website.

Expressing concerns over impact of poor land valuation on the RTI Act, Acharyulu said, "The Commission finds in many cases before it that several public authorities are escaping accountability under RTI by showing value of the land given to them by the government as 'commercial value' which is an open lie as every one knows the real value would be thousand times more than what it was shown to be."

He said several hospitals, sports clubs, cricket associations are claiming that the land was given to them at commercial rate, simply because the state does not have any document to say that they have properly assessed the value of the land in a particular area.

"Because of this every selfish person or profit motivated corporate body is trying to take prime government land using the corruption as an easy tool and making huge profits at the cost of public exchequer and imposing burden on common consumers," he said in the order.

The observations of the Commission came on a plea of an activist S P Manchanda who had given detailed description to Delhi government on the loopholes in the process to determine rates of land in various circles resulting in revenue loss.

Acharyulu said all this is facilitated by the absence of 'minimum governance' at the higher level where the powers that be prefer to relax and refuse to decide what is the value of the land.

Commenting on the verdict, RTI activist Subhash Agrawal, who is fighting for BCCI to be declared a public authority, said, "Huge Firoz Shah Kotla Stadium at capital's one of the most prime locations at Bahadurshah Zafar Marg has been given an exclusive circle-rate that too in a much lower 'C' category with just rupees 1,59,840 per square meter, rather than its being categorised in 'A' category with circle-rate of rupees 7,75,000 per sq m."

     Embrace Your Own Power to Fight Corruption

In his submission to Delhi Government in 2013, Manchanda had claimed that the circle rates have been wrongfully kept uniform all over the national capital which is resulting in serious revenue loss to the exchequer.

"Kesav Puram, market rate of an MIG flat is Rs 1.4 crore whereas the stamp duty collected on the basis of circle rate which is Rs 40 lakh thereby stamp duty on the value of Rs one crore is lost. Similarly in Narela, the value of flat is 15 lakh but the circle rate is as high as Rs 37 lakh on which the stamp duty is collected hence there are no buyers of the flats in that area," Manchanda had claimed giving an example.

He approached the Delhi Government seeking to know action taken on his suggestion but not getting satisfactory response he approached the Central Information Commission.

During the hearing, the Delhi Government representative accepted the anomaly and said a new section has been inserted in the Indian Stamps Act as a corrective measure.

Lauding Manchanda's efforts, Acharyulu termed the RTI application as "one of the best" in the interest of fulfilling the objectives of the Right to Information Act.

"A simple and ordinary person, Mr S P Manchanda is in fact, not seeking any information from the public authority but making a very constructive suggestion after pointing out how much of revenue the Government was loosing every day because of the indifference and delay in developing a rational valuation of land policy," he said.

NEWSROOM24X7 NETWORK

Central Information Commission asks Health Ministry and NPPA to check the menace of overpricing of essential drugs.

New Delhi

The Central Information Commission has recommended to the Union Ministry of Health and Family Welfare, Department of Pharmaceuticals and National Pharmaceutical Pricing Authority (NPPA) to initiate a coordinated attempt to address the issue of checking the menace of overpricing of essential drugs and excessive trade margins to promote greater transparency for the benefit of the common man within a period of 2 months.

Central Information Commissioner Bimal Julka passed a significant order on 1 October 2018 in response to an appeal under the RTI Act linked with overpricing of essential drugs. The order says the information sought with regard to the subject matter pertained to Union Health Ministry which also had a catalytic role to play in checking the menace of over pricing of essential drugs and excessive trade margins.

The Commission has observed that the larger issue relating to the price structure and extraordinary heavy trade margins on the medicines especially generic medicines had not been addressed by the Respondent. The Respondent (NPPA) present at the hearing expressed inability to intervene.

The Appellant, S. P. Manchanda, through his RTI application had sought information on 5 points regarding whether or not NPPA was aware that some oncology medicines required for treating cancer had MRP printed which was many times more than their ex-factory price or import price with much higher profit margin. If yes, steps taken by the Authority to regulate their prices

 Embrace Your Own Power to Fight Corruption

and action taken against manufacturers, importers, distributors and hospitals and doctors for looting the hapless patients, whether NPPA received complaints from the public or any other government organization or NGO on the aforementioned issue, details of the complainants who filed complaints during the last 5 years and the related issues.

The information sought by the appellant was in the larger public interest pertaining to the price regulation of oncology medicines required for treating cancer patients. It was submitted before the Commission that a cogent and clear response ought to have been provided by the Respondent instead of skirting around the issues and taking the plea of disproportionate diversion of resources in answering the application. The intervener Subhash Chandra Agrawal raised larger public interest issues regarding availability of essential drugs at inflated MRPs detrimental to the interests of the needy patients who suffer the most. It was argued that the Ministry of Health, Department of Pharmaceuticals and NPPA have not been able to check the perpetual escalation in prices of essential drugs at exaggerated MRPs. While technically, in accordance with the provisions of the RTI Act, 2005, the information may have been provided to the Appellant but the greater issue of the mental agony and harassment caused to the suffering patients for abnormally high prices of drugs remained unchecked.

The Respondent stated during the hearing that the information held and available with the Public Authority had been provided. While referring to the Drugs (Prices Control) Order, 2013 alongwith the National Pharmaceutical Pricing Policy, 2012, the Respondent submitted that the prices were regulated based on 1) Essentiality of drugs; 2) Control of formulations prices only and 3) Market based Pricing and that the "Essentiality" criteria for drugs under the NPPP- 2012 was to be met by considering the list of medicines specified in the National List of Essential

Medicines as revised from time to time and most recently declared by the Ministry of Health and Family Welfare, Government of India. The Respondent nonetheless continued to maintain that they were adhering to the Drugs (Prices Control) Order, 2013. It was further informed that the aspect of revision of ceiling price of the individual drugs or retail price of a pack was a decision to be taken in consultation with the Ministry of Health and that the efforts were underway to coordinate the same. It was specifically mentioned that a draft policy paper to determine the prices of a large number of essential drugs was under preparation in consultation with Ministry of Health and that the same would be notified in due course.

The Commission received a written submission from the Respondent on 25 September 2018, giving a point-wise response to the queries raised in the RTI application. For point no. 1, it was stated that pursuant to the announcement of the National Pharmaceutical Pricing Policy, 2012 (NPPP, 2012), the Govt. notified Drugs (Price Control) Order, 2013 on 15 May 2013. The medicines specified in the National List of Essential Medicines 2011 (NLEM) were included in the First Schedule of DPCO, 2013 and brought under price control. Further, the National List of Essential Medicines, 2015 was notified by the Ministry of Health and Family Welfare in December, 2015. It was thereafter notified as the First Schedule of DPCO, 2013 in March, 2016 by the Department of Pharmaceuticals. Accordingly, NPPA had fixed and notified ceiling prices of 851 scheduled formulations including 2 coronary stents and 81 cancer medicines under revised Schedule I (NLEM, 2015). It was further stated that the Government was effectively monitoring the prices of scheduled medicines notified by NLEM and appropriate action was taken against companies overcharging for the drugs. The details of the overcharging cases initiated by the NPPA were also available on its website. With regard to point no. 2, it was stated that compiling the information on the subject for the last 5 years from different sources and obtaining the third party consent would take substantial time and resources of their office which would be against the larger public interest. As regards point no. 3, it was stated that the information was never denied to the Appellant as he was informed about the website link to access NPPA recommendations on the issue. Explaining that being an attached office communication was not made directly with other ministers for policy related issues, it was stated that the physical copy of voluminous document was not provided along with the reply as RTI application was lodged online and applicant had never asked for the physical copy specifically. Regarding point no. 4, the status of Appellant's online grievance of 18 March 2018 was provided. Considering the difficulties associated with the compilation of information, the information about all other public grievances received through PG portal could not be provided. Regarding point no. 5, it was stated that the inspection was not required since the records relating to pricing of formulations and overcharging cases were available on the website of NPPA. Further the records were not static in nature and being updated from time to time. While explaining that the information asked by the Appellant was provided within the stipulated time period, it was stated that the status of complaint disposal was a continuous activity in a regulatory mechanism and the status of overcharged cases was disclosed to the public only when the case reached to conclusion such as issue of demand to company or the matter had been referred to the Collector for recovery.

The Commission even received an e-mail from Subhash Chandra Agrawal on 27 September 2018 stating that he was intimated about the matter on the eve of the hearing and submitted that since he was pre-occupied he wished to intervene in the matter of larger public interest through e-mail and if required through audio conference. Explaining that although the Appellant had raised important issue only with reference to cancer medicines but NPPA also ignored price structure and extra ordinary heavy trade margins on medicines especially generic medicines. Even though the matter was repeatedly taken up through various portals, yet NPPA ignored such suggestions. It was further submitted that his intervention application was also not irrelevant since cancer patients also consumed medicines other than the ones exclusively meant for them. Thus, it was submitted that his suggestions could be made part of CIC's verdict for recommendations, under the provisions of the RTI Act, 2005 including Section 25 (5) with a compliance report from NPPA in a time bound manner on the recommendations.

The Commission also received another written submission from Subhash Chandra Agrawal on 28 September 2018 with a prayer to direct the Respondent to place the matter before the concerned Ministers and Secretaries of the two concerned ministries for their personal attention apart from seeking the action taken reports and working sheets on the suggestions in a time bound period to achieve a noble public cause.

***

Disclose how ceiling prices of stents fixed: CIC to NPPA

February 22, 2017

New Delhi, Feb 22 (PTI) The Central Information Commission today directed the National Pharmaceutical Pricing Authority to disclose all records on the basis of which "ceiling prices" for the coronary stents were fixed.

The transparency watchdog also directed the NPPA to maintain catalogued data of all complaints bringing out instances of overcharging by hospitals along with action taken by it.

"Details of aforesaid complaints found true along with penal/corrective action taken by NPPA shall be proactively placed in public domain through the website of NPPA," Information Commissioner Yashovardhan Azad said in his order.

He said these directions are being issued under the powers conferred under Section 19(8)(a)(iv) of the RTI Act, 2005 to "promote greater transparency, which shall ensure that the benefits of beneficial executive actions reach the general masses".

The Section of the transparency law empowers the Commission to issue directives to any public authority to make necessary changes "to its practices in relation to the maintenance, management and destruction of records".

The order came on the plea of Suraj Prakash who had sought to know the basis on which the NPPA has fixed the prices of all types of coronary stents.

"The Commission is inclined to allow the request of the appellant considering the larger public interest involved... the CPIO shall also furnish complete information including notesheets along with the relevant documents/price costing estimations etc. whereupon the ceiling prices were arrived at by the NPPA," Azad said.

The issue of coronary stents came to media limelight following instructions issued by the government yesterday invoking an emergency clause under drug pricing control law thus making it mandatory for stent makers to maintain production and supply of coronary stents.

However, the matter before the Commission pertained to an RTI application filed on September 9, 2015.

The pharmaceutical department said there have been reports of shortage of coronary stents in the market and hospitals.

Last week, the government had slashed prices of stents by up to 85 per cent by capping them at Rs 7,260 for bare metal ones and Rs 29,600 for the drug eluting variety.

Under the Section 3 (i) of DPCO, 2013, the government can regulate distribution and direct any manufacturer to increase production and sell products to institutions, hospitals or any agency as the case may be in case of emergency or in circumstances of urgency or in case of non-commercial use in public interest.

***

A complaint was made to the CM regarding the black money being generated in the undervaluation of the properties in Delhi &Loss of revenue to the Govt- CIC: this application is one of the best in the interest of fulfilling the objectives of the RTI Act 8 Apr, 2015

Observation: One of the Best RTI Applications

1. The appellant is present. The Public Authority is represented by Mr. Lalit Mohan, SDM (HQ), Mr. MPS Rawat, NT.

Facts:

2. The Appellant through his RTI application dated 28.08.2013 had sought information with respect to his representation dated 10.08.2013 which was sent to

    Embrace Your Own Power to Fight Corruption

Hon'ble C.M – How to curb black money in property transactions and prevent corruption Viz

i.   Date of receipt of his representation by the office

ii.   status of its progress

iii.   Detail of the Official who handled the representation and the action taken by them

iv.   If No action, then the reason for the same, etc.

3. PIO vide his letter dated 23.09.2013 requested the appellant to meet the PIO and discuss the matter.

4. Being unsatisfied with the information furnished, the appellant preferred First Appeal.

5. FAA by his Order dated 03.01.2014 directed the SDMII to provide fresh reply to the appellant.

6. In Compliance of FAA Order, PIO requested the appellant to visit the office for discussing the matter.

7. Being unsatisfied with the information furnished, the appellant has approached the Commission in Second Appeal.

DECISION

8. Both the parties made their submissions. The appellant submitted that he had made a complaint dated 1082013 addressed to the Chief Minister of Delhi regarding the corruption and the black money being generated in the undervaluation of the properties in Delhi and loss of revenue to the Government. The Government has kept uniform circle rates all over Delhi, irrespective of the area, with the result the area in which the appellant is living, Kesav Puram, the market rate of an MIG Flat is

Rs. 1,40,00,000/ whereas the stamp duty is collected on the basis of circle rates, i.e. Rs. 40,00,000/ thereby losing the stamp duty on the value of Rs. One crore. Similarly, in Narela, the value of a flat is just Rs.15 lakhs, but the Circle rate is as high as Rs.37 lakhs, on which the stamp duty is assessed. Hence in Narela, there are no buyers for the flats.

9. On the other hand, the respondent officer, Mr. Lalit Mohan, SDM (Hq) submitted that the appellant's complaint contained allegations on the undervaluation of the properties in Delhi. The Government has constituted a Committee namely, Committee on Revision of Circle Rates 2014, and his representation was placed before that Committee. The respondent officer also admitted the anomaly pointed out by the appellant regarding the circle rates and submitted that the Government may soon set right this anomaly.

   Section 27 of the Indian Stamps Act deals with the undervaluation of the properties. A new section 47A has been inserted on 2392014 by amending the said Act, by which the Collector of Stamps has the power to assess the real value of the property, when the document is referred to him and enhance the same, if he considers there is undervaluation.

10. The Commission finds this RTI application is one of the best in the interest of fulfilling the objectives of the Right to Information Act. The Commission also found a relief after hearing plethora of misused RTI appeals filed by disgruntled employees or those facing disciplinary actions or caught red handed taking bribe, or facing challenge from wives for their cruelty. Most of these are guided by

   Embrace Your Own Power to Fight Corruption

self interest or private grudge or motivated by revenge or intended to harass and never with any public interest. A simple and ordinary person, Mr S P Manchanda is in fact, not seeking any information from the public authority but making a very constructive suggestion after pointing out how much of revenue the Government was loosing every day because of the indifference and delay in developing a rational valuation of land policy.

11. This RTI application is in its own way a small but effective suggestion to curb growth of black money and increase the state revenue with so many positive effects. He has approached the Chief Minister of Delhi with suggestion to curb black money and prevent corruption in property transactions in Delhi. He wanted to know the action taken on his representation. As usual the PIO gave some lifeless, routine reply saying you have just made a suggestion and did not ask for any information. Then advised him to come and inspect the files. The appellant called it vague and incomplete. In spite of the specific direction by the first appellate authority, information was not provided. In second appeal he sought a thorough enquiry against concealing of information, which he alleges to be mala fide. Appellant expressed disgust at the way he was made to take several trips to the offices in futility. He also sought costs for causing him mental agony and penalty for denial of information.

12. The appellant suggested how futile to decide uniform circle rates for entire Delhi without distinguishing the high value at one place and low value at another center. He gave examples how the state was losing lots of revenue every day

which also generate huge black money. The PIO who was present at the hearing appeared responsive and completely agreed with agonised presentation of the appellant.

13. The Commission finds in many cases before it that several public authorities are escaping accountability under RTI by showing value of the land given to them by the Government as 'commercial value' which is an open lie as every one knows the real value would be thousand times more than what it was shown to be. Several hospitals, sports clubs, Cricket Associations etc are claiming the land was given to them at commercial rate, simply because the state does not have any document to say that they have properly assessed the value of the land in a particular area. Because of this every selfish person or profit motivated corporate body is trying to take prime government land using the corruption as an easy tool and making huge profits at the cost of public exhequer and imposing burden on common consumers. All this is facilitated by the absence of minimum governance at the higher level where the powers that be prefer to relax and refuse to decide what is value of the land.

14. The Commission exercising its powers under Section 19(8) (a) In its decision, the Central Information Commission or State Information Commission, as the case may be, has the power to require the public authority to take any such steps as may be necessary to secure compliance with the provisions of this Act, including (i) by providing access to information, if so requested, in a particular form; (ii) by appointing a Central Public Information Officer or State Public Information Officer, as the case may be;

   Embrace Your Own Power to Fight Corruption

(iii) by publishing certain information or categories of information; (iv) by making necessary changes to its practices in relation to the maintenance, management and destruction of records; (v) by enhancing the provision of training on the right to information for its officials; (vi) by providing it with an annual report in compliance with clause (b) of sub-section (1) of section 4; require the top officer of the public authority, Chief Secretary of Government of Delhi, to take a serious look into the highly significant suggestions to decide the circle rates of land value in Delhi and for that initiate inquiry or if any inquiry is already ordered as informed by the PIO, expedite the proceedings of that inquiry.

15. The Commission directs the respondent authority to provide a copy of the report of the Committee on revision of Circle rates to the appellant, and also upload the same on the Web site, as and when report is ready. The appeal is disposed of accordingly with above observations. The registry is directed to send a copy of this order to the Chief Secretary and the Administrator of Delhi.

(M.Sridhar Acharyulu)

Information Commisisoner

Citation: Sh. S.P.Manchanda v. SDM (HQII) GNCTD in File No.CIC/SA/A/2014/000576

CIC wants Delhi government to reveal how circle rates were finalisedRumu Banerjee

Aug 28, 2017

NEW DELHI

The Delhi government's assertions of public participation in governance have been called out by the Central Information Commission (CIC).

In response to an RTI plea asking for details of suggestions taken on board by the AAP government while rationalisingcircle rates, information commissioner Yashovardhan Azad has directed the revenue department of the Delhi government to share the information with the appellant. The revenue department will thereafter have to submit a compliance report to the CIC, Azad ruled.

The order came on an RTI plea filed by S P Manchanda, who wanted to know if the Delhi government had acted on any suggestions by the public on rationalisation of circle rates after calling for such submissions in July last year.

Azad concurred with the appellant's arguments and said in his order, "The commission notes that this is an important issue and one which addresses a public cause. Accordingly, the respondent is directed to provide response to the queries of the appellant and allow inspection of all relevant records within three weeks of receipt of this order."

Manchanda, who had filed his RTI application in February, had submitted suggestions to the revenue department, which had come out with an advertisement in some newspapers in July 2016. The suggestions, which were sought by the Delhi government to rationalise circle rates, were to be submitted by August.

Manchanda, however, didn't receive any response to his RTI plea, and approached the CIC.

Azad's order said, "Appellant states that discrepancy between circle rates and market valuation is leading to huge loss to public exchequer since legal transfer of such properties is discouraged and no clear information in this regard is made accessible due to deliberate concealment."

HC REJECTS PLEA TO CUT COURT HOLIDAYS: OVERWORKED,WHY DENY US VACATION

July 4, 2013

A PIL seeking reduction in the duration of court vacations and cancellation of the month-long summer break in the Delhi High Court prompted the Acting Chief Justice to ask the petitioner why he was against holidays for judges.

Written by Aneesha Mathur | New Delhi | Published: July 4, 2013 1:37:59 am

A PIL seeking reduction in the duration of court vacations and cancellation of the month-long summer break in the Delhi High Court prompted the Acting Chief Justice to ask the petitioner why he was against holidays for judges. The petitioner said vacations should be curtailed so that a large number of pending cases could be dealt with.

We will examine the issue but why are you against our holidays?"Acting Chief Justice Badar Durrez Ahmed asked petitioner S P Manchanda, president of NGO Prakash India,who had appeared in person to argue the case.

The petitioner said long summer vacations "infringed on the fundamental right of the people to get speedy justice and was violative of Articles 14 and 21 of the Constitution.

The PIL sought orders to "discontinue the summer vacations

     Embrace Your Own Power to Fight Corruption

of the High Court of Delhi" and to "curtail vacations of the Delhi High Court by 10 to 15 days as recommended by the Law Commission of India.

The petitioner argued that courts had huge arrears of cases, and several thousand cases were pending before the Delhi High Court. The solution, he said, was to increase working hours and reduce the vacation time of the courts.

"En bloc summer vacations are a concept introduced by the British who found the Indian summer unbearable. Why should it continue now when we have ACs and other technology that makes working in the summer easy? Manchanda argued.

The bench of Acting Chief Justice Ahmed and Justice Vibhu Bakhru dismissed the plea: Judges and lawyers are already overworked and cannot be required to work anymore than they already are. If the court is sitting in rotation, when will lawyers get a break?"

The petitioner was told that the Delhi High Court was "religiously following Central government rules mandating 210 court-sitting days and that judges had to do a lot of work even when they were not sitting in the courtrooms".

"Most judges do not spend their summer vacations vacationing but spend time in their office at home or in High Court writing judgments," the bench said.

"Perhaps the petitioner does not know that even in summer vacation,the court is not closed for those who are in urgent need. Vacation benches sit every Monday, Wednesday and Friday," the bench said.

Notes:

Embrace Your Own Power to Fight Corruption

Notes: